Virgin Saints and Martyrs

S. Baring-Gould

Virgin Saints and Martyrs

ISBN: 978-1-64799-610-9

CONTENTS

I

BLANDINA THE SLAVE

In the second century Lyons was the Rome of Gaul as it is now the second Paris of France. It was crowded with temples and public monuments. It was moreover the Athens of the West, a resort of scholars. Seated at the confluence of two great rivers, the Rhône and the Sâone, it was a centre of trade. It is a stately city now. It was more so in the second century when it did not bristle with the chimneys of factories pouring forth their volumes of black smoke, which the atmosphere, moist from the mountains, carries down so as to envelop everything in soot.

In the great palace, now represented by the hospital, the imbecile Claudius and the madman Caligula were born. To the east and south far away stand Mont Blanc and the snowy range on the Dauphiné Alps.

Lyons is a city that has at all times summed in it the finest as well as the worst characteristic of the Gallic people. The rabble of Lyons were ferocious in 177, and ferocious again in 1793; but at each epoch, during the Pagan terror and the Democratic terror, it produced heroes of faith and endurance.

The Emperor Marcus Aurelius was a philosopher full of good intentions, and a sentimental lover of virtue. But he fondly conceived that virtue could only be found in philosophy, and that Christianity, which was a doctrine and not a speculation, must be wrong; and as its chief adherents belonged to the slave and needy classes, that therefore it was beneath his dignity to inquire into it. He was a stickler for the keeping up of old Roman institutions, and the maintenance of such rites as were sanctioned by antiquity; and because the Christians refused to give homage to the gods and to swear by the genius of the emperor, he ordered that they should be persecuted to the death.

5He had been a pretty, curly-haired boy, and a good-looking young man. He had kept himself respectable, and looked on himself with smug self-satisfaction accordingly. Had he stooped to inquire what were the tenets, and what the lives, of those whom he condemned to death, he would have shrunk with horror from the guilt of proclaiming a general persecution.

In Lyons, as elsewhere, when his edict arrived the magistrates were bound to seek out and sentence such as believed in Christ.

A touching letter exists, addressed by the Church of Lyons to

1

those of Asia and Phrygia giving an account of what it suffered; and as the historian Eusebius embodied it in his history, it happily has been preserved from the fingering, and rewriting, and heightening with impossible marvels which fell to the lot of so many of the Acts of the Martyrs, when the public taste no longer relished the simple food of the unadorned narratives that were extant.

"The grace of God," said the writers, "contended for us, rescuing the weak, and 6strengthening the strong. These latter endured every species of reproach and torture. First they sustained bravely all the insults heaped on them by the rabble—blows and abuse, plundering of their goods, stoning and imprisonment. Afterwards they were led into the forum and were questioned by the tribune and by the town authorities before all the people, and then sent to prison to await the coming of the governor. Vetius Epagathus, one of the brethren, abounding in love to God and man, offered to speak in their defence; whereupon those round the tribunal shouted out at him, as he was a man of good position. The governor did not pay attention to his request, but merely asked whether he, too, were a Christian. When he confessed that he was, he also was transferred to the number of the martyrs."

What the numbers were we are not told. The most prominent among them were Pothinus, the bishop, a man in his ninetieth year, Sanctus, the deacon of the Church of Vienne, Maturus, a recent convert, Attalus, a native of Pergamus, Blandina, a slave girl, 7and her mistress, another woman named Biblis, and Vetius, above referred to.

Among those arrested were ten who when tortured gave way: one of these was Biblis; but, although they yielded, yet they would not leave the place of trial, and remained to witness the sufferings of such as stood firm; and some—among these was Biblis—plucking up courage, presented themselves before the judge and made amends for their apostasy by shedding their blood for Christ.

The slaves belonging to the Christians of rank had been seized and were interrogated; and they, in their terror lest they should be put to torture, confessed anything the governor desired—that the Christians ate little children and "committed such crimes as are neither lawful for us to speak of nor think about; and which we really believe no men ever did commit."

The defection of the ten caused dismay among the faithful, for they feared lest it should be the prelude to the surrender of others.

The governor, the proconsul, arrived at the 8time of the annual fair, when Lyons was crowded; and he deemed this a good opportunity for striking terror into the hearts of the Christians.

2

Those who stood firm were brought out of prison, and, as they would not do sacrifice to the gods, were subjected to torture.

Blandina was a peculiarly delicately framed young woman, and not strong. Her mistress, who was one of the martyrs, was apprehensive for her; but Blandina in the end witnessed the most splendid confession of all. She was frightfully tortured with iron hooks and hot plates applied to her flesh from morning till night, till the executioners hardly knew what more to do; "her entire body being torn and pierced."

Brass plates, red hot, were also applied to the most tender parts of the body of the deacon, Sanctus, but he continued unsubdued, firm in his confession. At last he was thrown down on the sand, a mass of wounds, so mangled and burnt that he seemed hardly to retain the human shape. He and Blandina were conveyed back to prison.

Next day "the tormentors tortured Sanctus again, supposing that whilst his wounds were swollen and inflamed, if they continued to rend them when so sensitive as not to bear the touch of the hand, they must break his spirit"—but it was again in vain.

Then it was that Biblis, the woman who had done sacrifice, came forward "like one waking out of a deep sleep," and upbraided the torturers; whereupon she was dragged before the chief magistrate, confessed Christ, and was numbered among the martyrs.

The proconsul ordered all to be taken back to prison, and they were thrust into a black and noisome hole, and fastened in the stocks, their feet distended to the fifth hole—that is to say, stretched apart as far as was possible without dislocation—and so, covered with sores, wounds and blisters, unable to sleep in this attitude, they were left for the night. The suffocation of the crowded den was too much for some, and in the morning certain of those who had been crowded into it were drawn forth dead.

Next day the aged bishop Pothinus was led before the magistrate. He was questioned, and asked who was the God of the Christians.

"If thou art worthy," answered he, "thou shalt know."

He was then stripped and scourged, and beaten about the head. The crowd outside the barriers now took up whatever was at hand, stones, brickbats, dirt, and flung them at him, howling curses and blasphemies. The old man fell gasping, and in a state hardly conscious was dragged to the prison.

And now, on the great day of the fair, when the shows were to be given to the people, the proconsul for their delectation threw open the amphitheatre. This was a vast oval, capable of holding

3

forty thousand spectators. It was packed. On one side, above the arena, was the seat of the chief magistrate, and near him those reserved for the city magnates. At the one end, a series of arches, now closed with gates of stout bars and cross-bars, hinged above and raised on these hinges by a chain, opened from the dens in which the wild beasts were kept. The beasts had not been fed for three days, that they might be ravenous.

It was the beginning of June—doubtless a bright summer day, and an awning kept off the sun from the proconsul. Those on one side of the amphitheatre, the slaves on the highest row, could see, vaporous and blue on the horizon, above the crowded tiers opposite, the chain of the Alps, their crests white with eternal snows.

"No sooner was the chief magistrate seated, to the blare of trumpets, than the martyrs were introduced. Sanctus had to be supported; he could hardly walk, he was such a mass of wounds. All were now stripped of their garments and were scourged. Blandina was attached to a post in the centre of the arena. She had been forced every day to attend and witness the sufferings of the rest."

But even now they were not to be despatched at once. Maturus and Sanctus were placed on iron chairs, and fires were lighted under them so that the fumes of their roasted flesh rose up and were dissipated by the light summer air over the arena, and the sickening savour was inhaled by the thousands of cruel and savage spectators.

Then they were cast off to be despatched with the sword.

The dens were opened. Lions, tigers, leopards bounded forth on the sand roaring. By a strange accident Blandina escaped. The hungry beasts paced round the arena, but would not touch her.

Then a Greek physician, called Alexander, who was looking on, unable to restrain his enthusiasm, by signs gave encouragement to the martyrs. So at least it would seem, for all at once we learn that the mob roared for Alexander, as one who urged on the Christians to obstinacy. The governor sent for him, asked who he was, and when he confessed that he was a Christian, sent him to prison.

Attalus was now led forth, with a tablet on his breast on which was written in Latin, "This is Attalus, the Christian."

As he was about to be delivered to the tormentors, some one whispered to the proconsul that the man was a Roman. He hesitated, and sent him back to prison.

Then a number of other Christians who had Roman citizenship were produced, and had their heads struck off. Others who had not this privilege were delivered over to the beasts. And now some of those who had recanted came forward and offered themselves to death.

4

Next day the proconsul was again in his place in the amphitheatre. He had satisfied himself that Attalus could not substantiate his claim to citizenship, so he ordered him to torture and death. He also was placed in the iron chair; after which he and Alexander were given up to be devoured by the beasts.

This was the last day of the shows, and to crown all, Blandina was now produced, together with a boy of fifteen, called Ponticus. He, like Blandina, had been compelled daily to witness the torments to which the rest had been subjected.

And now the same hideous round of tortures began, and Blandina in the midst of her agony continued to encourage the brave boy till he died. Blandina had been roasted in the iron chair and scourged.

As a variety she was placed in a net. Then the gate of one of the larger dens was raised, and forth rushed a bull, pawed the sand, tossed his head, looked round, and seeing the net, plunged forward with bowed head. Next moment Blandina was thrown into the air, fell, was thrown again, then gored—but was happily now unconscious. Thus she died, and "even the Gentiles confessed that no woman among them had ever endured sufferings as many and great." But not even then was their madness and cruelty to the saints satisfied, for "... those who were suffocating in prison were drawn forth and cast to the dogs; and they watched night and day over the remains left by beasts and fire, however mangled they might be, to prevent us from burying them. The bodies, after exposure and abuse in every possible way during six days, were finally cast into the Rhône. These things they did as if they were able to resist God and prevent their resurrection."

The dungeons in which S. Pothinus, S. Blandina, and the rest of the martyrs were kept through so many days, are shown beneath the abbey church of Ainay at Lyons. It is possible enough that Christian tradition may have preserved the remembrance of the site. They are gloomy cells, without light or air, below the level of the river. The apertures by which they are entered are so low that the visitor is obliged to creep into them on his hands and knees. Traces of Roman work remain. Adjoining is a crypt that was used as a chapel till the Revolution, when it was desecrated. It is, however, again restored, the floor has been inlaid with mosaics, and the walls are covered with modern frescoes, representing the passion of the martyrs.

What makes it difficult to believe that these are the dungeons is that the abbey above them is constructed on the site of the Athenæum founded by Caligula, a great school of debate and composition, and it is most improbable that the town prisons should have been under the university buildings. In all likelihood in the early Middle Ages these vaults were found and supposed to have been the prisons of the martyrs, and supposition very rapidly became assurance that they were so. The prison in which the martyrs were enclosed was the lignum or robur, which was certainly not below the level of the river.

The question arises, when one reads stories of such inhuman cruelties done, did the victims suffer as acutely as we suppose? I venture to think not at the time. There can be no question, as it is a thing repeatedly attested, that in a moment of great excitement the nerves are not very sensitive. The pain of wounds received in battle is not felt till after the battle is over. Moreover, it may be questioned whether the human system can endure pain above a certain grade—whether, in fact, beyond a limit, insensibility does not set in.

I attended once a poor lady who was frightfully burnt. A paraffin lamp set fire to a gauze or lace wrap she had about her neck. All her throat and the lower portion of her face were frightfully burnt. I was repeatedly with her, but she was unconscious or as in a sleep; there was no expression of anguish in her face. She quietly sank through exhaustion. I have questioned those who have met with shocking accidents, and have always been assured that the pain began when nature commenced its labour of repair. Pain, excruciating pain, can be endured, and for a long period; but I think that when carried beyond a fixed limit it ceases to be appreciable, as insensibility sets in.

This is a matter for investigation, and it were well if those who read these lines were to endeavour to collect evidence to substantiate or overthrow what is, with me, only an opinion.

II

S. CÆCILIA

In 1876, when I was writing the November volume of my "Lives of the Saints," and had to deal with the Acts of S. Cæcilia, I saw at once that they were eminently untrustworthy—they were, in fact, a religious romance, very similar to others of the like nature; and my mistrust was deepened when I found that the name of Cæcilia did not appear in either the Roman Kalendar of the fourth century, nor in the Carthagenian of the fifth.

The Acts were in Greek, and it was not till the time of Pope Gelasius (496) that her name appeared at all prominently; then he introduced it into his Sacramentary.

The Acts as we have them cannot be older than the fifth century, and contain gross anachronisms. They make her suffer when Urban was Pope, under an apocryphal prefect, Turcius Almachius; but the date of Pope Urban was in the reign of Alexander Severus, who did not persecute the Church at all—who, in fact, favoured the Christians.

But although there is so much to make one suspicious as to the very existence of S. Cæcilia, a good many facts have been brought to light which are sufficient to show that it was the stupidity of the composer of the apocryphal Acts which has thrown such doubt over the Virgin Martyr.

If we eliminate what is obviously due to the romantic imagination of the author of the Acts in the fifth century, the story reduces itself to this.

Cæcilia was a maiden of noble family, and her parents were of senatorial rank. From her earliest youth she was brought up as a Christian, but that her father was one is doubtful, as he destined his daughter to become the wife of an honourable young patrician named Valerian, who was, however, a pagan.

Cæcilia would not hear of the marriage on this account; and Valerian, who loved her dearly, by her advice went to Urban the Pope, who was living in concealment in the Catacomb in the Appian Way, to learn something about the Faith. Valerian took with him his brother, Tiburtius; they were both convinced, were baptised, and, as they confessed Christ, suffered martyrdom; and the officer who arrested them, named Maximus, also believed and underwent the same fate. All three were laid in the Catacomb of Prætextatus.

Cæcilia, in the meantime, had remained unmolested in her father's house in Rome.

The Prefect resolved to have her put to death privately, as she belonged to an illustrious family, perhaps also in consideration for her father, still a heathen.

He gave orders that the underground passages for heating the winter apartments should be piled with wood, and an intense fire made, and that the room in which Cæcilia was should be closed, so that she should die of suffocation. This was done, but she survived the attempt. This is by no means unlikely. The walls were heated by pipes through which the hot air passed, and there was a thick pavement of concrete and mosaic between the fires and the room. Everything depended on the chamber being shut up, and there being no air admitted; but it is precisely this latter requisite that could not be assured. In her own house, where the slaves were warmly attached to her, nothing would be easier than to withdraw the cover of the opening in the ceiling, by means of which ventilation was secured. By some means or other air was admitted, and although, doubtless, Cæcilia suffered discomfort from the great heat, yet she was not suffocated.

The chamber was the Calidarium, or hot-air bath attached to the palace, and in the church of S. Cæcilia in Trastevere a portion of this is still visible.

As the attempt had failed, the Prefect sent an executioner to kill her with the sword.

Her beauty, youth, and grace, so affected the man that, although he smote thrice at her throat, he did not kill her. It was against the law to strike more than thrice, so he left her prostrate on the mosaic floor bathed in her blood.

No sooner was the executioner gone than from all sides poured in her relatives, the slaves, and the faithful to see her, and to receive the last sigh of the Martyr. They found her lying on the marble pavement, half conscious only, and they dipped their kerchiefs in her blood, and endeavoured to staunch the wounds in her throat.

She lingered two days and nights in the same condition, and without moving, hanging between life and death; and then—so say the Acts—Pope Urban arrived, braving the risk, from his hiding-place, to say farewell to his dear daughter in the Faith. Thereupon she turned to him, commended to him the care of the poor, entreated her father to surrender his house to the Church, and expired. In the Acts she addresses the Pope as "Your Beatitude," an expression used in the fifth century, and certainly not in the third.

She died, as she had lain, her face to the ground, her hands and arms declining on the right, as she rested on that side.

The same night her body was enclosed in a cypress chest, and was conveyed to the cemetery of S. Callixtus, where Urban laid it in a chamber "near that in which reposed his brother prelates and martyrs."

So far the legend. Now let us see whether it is possible to reconcile it with history.

In the first place, it is to be observed that the whole of the difficulty lies with Urban being Pope. If we suppose that in the original Acts the name was simply "Urban the Bishop," and that the remodeller of the Acts took the liberty of transforming him into Pope Urban, the difficulty vanishes at once. He may have been some regionary bishop in hiding. He may not have been a bishop at all, but a priest; and the writer, ignorant of history, and knowing only of the Urbans as Popes, may have given rise to all this difficulty by transforming him into a Pope.

Now, in the Acts, the Prefect does not speak of the Emperor, but of "Domini nostri invictissimi principes" (our Lords the unconquered Princes). The Emperor, therefore, cannot have been Alexander. Now, Ado the martyrologist, in or about 850, must have referred to other Acts than those we possess, for he enters S. Cæcilia as having suffered under Marcus Aurelius and Commodus—that is to say, in 177. This explains the Prefect referring to the orders of the Princes.

If we take this as the date, and Urban as being a priest or bishop of the time, the anachronisms are at an end.

That the Acts should have been in Greek is no proof that they were not drawn up in Rome, for Greek was the language of the Church there, and indeed the majority of the most ancient inscriptions in the Catacombs are in that language.

So much for the main difficulties. Now let us see what positive evidences we have to substantiate the story.

The excavation of the Cemetery of S. Callixtus, which was begun in 1854, and was carried on with great care by De Rossi, led to the clearing out of a crypt in which the early Bishops of Rome had been laid. The bodies had been removed when Paschal I. conveyed so many of those of the saints and martyrs into Rome, on account of the ruin into which the Catacombs had fallen, but their epitaphs remained, all of the third century, and in Greek; among these, that of Urbanus, and it was perhaps precisely this fact which led the recomposer of the Acts to confound the Urban of S. Cæcilia's time with the Pope. The first Pope known to have been laid there was Zephyrinus, in 218. Here also was found an inscription set up by

Damasus I., recording how that the bodies of bishops and priests, virgins and confessors lay in that place.

Now by a narrow, irregular opening in the rock, entrance is obtained to a further chamber, about twenty feet square, lighted by a luminare in the top, or an opening to the upper air cut in the tufa. This, there can be no manner of doubt, is the crypt in which reposed the body of S. Cæcilia.

In the Acts it was said to adjoin that in which were laid the Bishops of Rome; though, as these bishops were of later date than Cæcilia, if we take her death to have been in 177, their crypt must have been dug out or employed for the purpose of receiving their bodies at a later period.

Again, it is an interesting fact, that here a number of the tombstones that have been discovered bear the Cæcilian name, showing that this cemetery must have belonged to that gens or clan. Not only so, but one is inscribed with that of Septimus Prætextatus Cæcilianus, a servant of God during thirty years. It will be remembered that Prætextatus was the name of the brother of Valerian, who was betrothed to Cæcilia, and it leads one to suspect that the families of Valerian and of Cæcilia were akin.

The chapel or crypt contains frescoes. In the luminare is painted a female figure with the hands raised in prayer. Beneath this a cross with a lamb on each side. Below are three male figures with the names Sebastianus, Curinus (Quirinus), and Polycamus. Sebastian is doubtless the martyr of that name whose basilica is not far off. Quirinus, who has the corona of a priest, is the bishop and martyr of Siscia, whose body was brought in 420 to Rome. Of Polycamus nothing is known, save that his relics were translated in the ninth century to S. Prassede.

Against the wall lower down is a seventh-century representation of S. Cæcilia, richly clothed with necklace and bracelets; below a head of Christ of Byzantine type, and a representation of S. Urban. But these paintings, which are late, have been applied over earlier decoration; behind the figure of S. Cæcilia is mosaic, and that of Christ is painted on the old porphyry panelling. There are in this crypt recesses for the reception of bodies, and near the entrance an arched place low enough to receive a sarcophagus; and there are traces as though the face had at one time been walled up.

The walls are covered with graffiti, or scribbles made by pilgrims. An inscription also remains, to state that this was the sepulchre of S. Cæcilia the Martyr, but this inscription is not earlier than the ninth or tenth century.

In 817 Paschal I. was Pope, and in the following year he

removed enormous numbers of the remains of martyrs from the Catacombs into the churches of Rome, because the condition into which these subterranean cemeteries were falling was one of ruin. They had been exposed to the depredations of the Lombards, and then to decay. Some had fallen in, and were choked.

Precisely this Catacomb had been plundered by the Lombard king, Astulf, and it was not known whether he had carried off the body of S. Cæcilia or not. All those of the former popes Paschal removed.

In 844, however, Paschal pretended that he had seen S. Cæcilia in a dream, who had informed him that she still lay in her crypt in the Catacomb of S. Callixtus. No reliance can be placed on the word of a man so unprincipled as Paschal. At this very time two men of the highest rank, who were supporters of Louis the Pious, the Emperor, had been seized, dragged to the Lateran Palace, their eyes plucked out, and then beheaded. The Pope was openly accused of this barbarous act. The Emperor sent envoys to examine into it, but Paschal threw all sorts of difficulties in their way. He refused to produce the murderers; he asserted that they were guilty of no crime in killing these unfortunate men, and he secured the assassins by investing them with a half-sacred character as servants of the Church of S. Peter. Himself he exculpated from all participation in the deed by a solemn, expurgatorial oath. Such was the man who pretended to visions of the saints. His dream was an afterthought. In the clearing out of the crypt of S. Cæcilia, the wall that had closed the grave was broken through, and the cypress chest was disclosed. Whereupon Paschal promptly declared he had dreamt that so it would be found. The body was found in the coffin, incorrupt, and at its feet were napkins rolled together and stained with blood.

This discovery, which seems wholly improbable, is yet not impossible. If the arcosolium had been hermetically sealed up, the body need not have fallen to dust; and, as a fact, De Rossi did discover, along with Marchi, in 1853, a body in the Via Appia, without the smallest trace of alteration and decay in the bones.[1]

Paschal himself relates that he lined the chest with fringed silk, and covered the body with a silk veil. It was then enclosed in a sarcophagus of white marble, and laid under the high altar of the Church of S. Cæcilia in Trastevere.

This church has been made out of the old house of S. Cæcilia, and to this day, notwithstanding rebuildings, it bears traces of its origin.

Nearly eight hundred years after this translation, Sfondrati,

---

[1] Rom. Sott. ii. 125.

11

cardinal of S. Cæcilia, being about to carry on material alterations in the basilica, came on the sarcophagus lying in a vault under the altar. It was not alone—another was with it.

In the presence of witnesses one of these was opened. It contained a coffin or chest of cypress wood. The Cardinal himself removed the cover. First was seen the costly lining and the silken veil, with which nearly eight centuries before Paschal had covered the body. It was faded, but not decayed, and through the almost transparent texture could be seen the glimmer of the gold of the garments in which the martyr was clad. After a pause of a few minutes, the Cardinal lifted the veil, and revealed the form of the maiden martyr lying in the same position in which she had died on the floor of her father's hall. Neither Urban nor Paschal had ventured to alter that. She lay there, clothed in a garment woven with gold thread, on which were the stains of blood; and at her feet were the rolls of linen mentioned by Paschal, as found with the body. She was lying on her right side, the arms sunk from the body, her face turned to the ground; the knees slightly bent and drawn together. The attitude was that of one in a deep sleep. On the throat were the marks of the wounds dealt by the clumsy executioner.

Thus she had lain, preserved from decay through thirteen centuries.

When this discovery was made, Pope Clement VIII. was lying ill at Frascati, but he empowered Cardinal Baronius and Bosio, the explorer of the Catacombs, to examine into the matter; and both of these have left an account of the condition in which the body was found. For five weeks all Rome streamed to the church to see the body; and it was not until S. Cæcilia's Day that it was again sealed up in its coffin and marble sarcophagus.

Cardinal Sfondrati gave a commission to the sculptor Maderna to reproduce the figure of the Virgin Martyr in marble in the attitude in which found, and beneath this is the inscription:— "So I show to you in marble the representation of the most holy Virgin Cæcilia, in the same position in which I myself saw her incorrupt lying in her sepulchre."

A woodcut was published at the time of the discovery figuring it, but this is now extremely scarce.

In the second sarcophagus were found the bones of three men; two, of the same age and size, had evidently died by decapitation. The third had its skull broken, and the abundant hair was clotted with blood, as though the martyr had been beaten to death and his skull fractured with the plumbatæ or leaded scourges.

The Acts of S. Cæcilia expressly say that this was the manner of death of Maximus. The other two bodies were doubtless those of Valerian and Tiburtius.

Of the statue by Maderna, Sir Charles Bell says: "The body lies on its side, the limbs a little drawn up; the hands are delicate and fine—they are not locked, but crossed at the wrists; the arms are stretched out. The drapery is beautifully modelled, and modestly covers the limbs.... It is the statue of a lady, perfect in form, and affecting from the resemblance to reality in the drapery of the white marble, and the unspotted appearance of the statue altogether. It lies as no living body could lie, and yet correctly, as the dead when left to expire—I mean in the gravitation of the limbs."

S. Cæcilia is associated with music: she is regarded as the patroness of the organ. This is entirely due to the highly imaginative Acts of the Fifth and Sixth Century.

> "Orpheus could lead the savage race;
> And trees uprooted left their place,
> Sequacious of the lyre:
> But bright Cæcilia rais'd the wonder higher:
> When to her organ vocal breath was given,
> An angel heard, and straight appear'd,
> Mistaking earth for heaven."

So sang Dryden. Chaucer has given the Legend of S. Cæcilia as the Second Nun's Tale in the Canterbury Pilgrimage.

There is a marvellous collection of ancient statues in Rome, in the Torlonia Gallery. It was made by the late Prince Torlonia. Unhappily, he kept three sculptors in constant employ over these ancient statues, touching them up, adding, mending, altering. It is a vast collection, and now the Torlonia family desire to sell it; but no one will buy, for no one can trust any single statue therein; no one knows what is ancient and what is new. The finest old works are of no value, because of the patching and correcting to which they have been subjected.

It is the same with the Acts of the Martyrs: they have been tinkered at and "improved" in the fifth and sixth centuries, and even later, no doubt with the best intention, but with the result that they have—or many of them have—lost credit altogether.

What a buyer of statuary from the Torlonia Gallery would insist on doing, would be to drag the statues out into the sunshine and go over them with a microscope and see where a piece of marble had been added, or where a new face had been put on old work. Then he would be able to form a judgment as to the value of the statue or bust. And this is precisely the treatment to which the legends of the martyrs have to be subjected. But this treatment tells sometimes in their favour. Narratives that at first sight seem conspicuously false or manufactured, will under the critical microscope reveal the sutures, and show what is old and genuine, and what is adventitious and worthless.

III

S. AGNES

About a mile from the Porta Pia, beside the Nomentine road that leads from Rome to the bridge over the Arno and to Montana, are the basilica and catacomb of S. Agnese. We are there on high ground, and here the parents of the saint had a villa and vineyard.

They were Christians, and their garden had an entrance to a catacomb in which the faithful were interred. We know this, because some of the burials in the passages underground are of more ancient date than the martyrdom of S. Agnes, which took place in 304.

A little lane, very dirty, leads down hence into the Salarian road, and there is a mean dribble of a stream in a hollow below.

The rock is all of the volcanic tufa that is so easily cut, but which in the roads resolves itself into mud of the dirtiest and most consistent description.

New Rome is creeping along the road, its gaunt and eminently vulgar houses are destroying the beauty of this road, which commanded exquisite views of the Sabine and Alban mountains, and the lovely Torlonia gardens have already been destroyed. Nor is this all, for the foundations of these useless and hideous buildings are being driven down into more than one old catacomb, which as soon as revealed is destroyed.

Where now stands the basilica of S. Agnese was the catacomb in which her body was laid. The church is peculiar, in that it is half underground. One has to descend into it by a staircase of forty-five ancient marble steps, lined with inscriptions taken from the catacomb. The cause for this peculiarity is not that the soil has risen about the basilica, but that when it was proposed to build the church over the tomb of the saint who was below in the catacomb, the whole of the crust of rock and earth above was removed, so that the subterranean passages were exposed to light; and then the foundations of the sacred edifice were laid on this level, and were carried up above the surface of the ground.

But this is not the only church that bears the name of S. Agnes: there is another in Rome itself, opposite the Torre Mellina, on the site of her martyrdom, in the Piazza Navona, which occupies the place of the old circus of Domitian. It is a very ugly building of 1642, but contains a tolerable representation, in relief, of the martyrdom of the saint.

15

Unfortunately we have not got the Acts of the martyrdom of S. Agnes in their original form. It was the custom of the Church to have scribes present at the interrogation and death of a martyr, who took down in shorthand the questions put and the answers made, and the sentence of the judge. These records, which were of the highest value, were preserved in the archives of the Roman Church. Unhappily, at a later age, such very simple accounts, somewhat crude maybe in style, and entirely deficient in the miraculous, did not suit the popular taste. Meanwhile the stories of the martyrs had been passed from mouth to mouth, and various additions had been made to give them a smack of romance; the account of the deaths was embellished with marvels, and made excruciating by the piling up of tortures; and then the popular voice declared that the persecutors must have been punished at once; so it was fabled that lightning fell and consumed them, or that the earth opened and swallowed them.

Now, when the Acts of Martyrs were found to contain nothing of all this, then writers set to work—not with the intention of deceiving, but with the idea that the genuine Acts were defective—to recompose the stories, by grafting into the original narrative all the rubbish that had passed current in popular legend. Thus it has come to pass that so few of the Acts of the Martyrs, as we have them, are in their primitive form. They have been more or less stuffed out with fabulous matter.

The Acts of S. Agnes are in this condition, although not so grossly meddled with as some others have been. That she was a real martyr, and that the broad outlines of her story are true, there can be no doubt.

The martyrdom took place during the reign of Diocletian.

In 304 he was in Italy. He had come to Rome the preceding year to celebrate the twentieth year of the reign of his colleague, Maximian, and at the same time the triumph over the Persians. He left Rome in ill humour at the independence of the citizens, after having been accustomed to the servility of the Easterns; the day was December 20th, and he went to Ravenna. The weather was cold and wet, and he was chilled, so that he suffered all the rest of the winter, and became irritable as his health failed. However, he went back to Rome; and at this time several martyrdoms ensued, as that of S. Soteris, a virgin of the noble family from which sprang S. Ambrose, also the boy Pancras, and S. Sebastian. But the most notable was Agnes.

She was aged only thirteen, and was the daughter of noble and wealthy parents, who were, as already said, Christians.

Her riches and beauty induced the son of a former prefect to

16

seek her hand in marriage. Agnes, however, refused. She had no desire to become a wife; at all events, at so early an age; and, moreover, she would on no account be united to a pagan. "I am already engaged to One," she said: "to Him I shall ever keep my troth."

Not understanding what she meant, he inquired further; and she is reported to have replied in an allegorical strain: "He has already bound me to Him by His betrothal ring, and has adorned me with precious jewels. He has placed a sign upon my brow that I should love none as I love Him. He has revealed unto me treasures incomparable, which He has promised to give me if I persevere. Honey and milk has He bestowed on me by His words. I have partaken of His body, and with His blood has He adorned my cheeks."

It must not, however, be supposed that this was actually what she said. There was then no scribe present to take the sentences down; they are words put into her mouth at a later period by a romance writer.

The young man was incensed, and complained to her father, who would in no way force his daughter's inclinations. The youth, unquestionably, did not understand her, and supposed that she had already given her heart to some earthly lover.

Presently it all came out. Agnes was a Christian, and, as a Christian, would not listen to his suit.

Then, in a rage, the young man rushed off and denounced her to the prefect, who sent immediately for her parents, and threatened them. They were weak in the faith; and, returning home trembling, urged their daughter to accept the youth. She, however, steadfastly refused.

There was now nothing for it but for her to appear before the Prefect of Rome. She stood before his tribunal with calmness and confidence.

"Come," said he, "be not headstrong: you are only a child, remember, though forward for your age."

"I may be a child," replied Agnes; "but faith does not depend on years, but on the heart."

The prefect presently lost his temper, and declared roundly: "I will tell you what shall be done with you; you shall be stripped and driven naked forth to the jeers and insults of the rabble."

Then the clothes were taken off the slender body of the girl. Thereupon she loosened the band that confined her abundant golden hair, and it fell in waves over her body and covered her to the knees.

"You may expose me to insult," said she; "but I have the angel

17

of God as my defence. For the only-begotten Son of God, whom you know not, will be to me an impenetrable wall and a guardian; never sleeping, and an unflagging protector."

"Let her be bound," ordered the judge, sullenly.

Then the executioner turned over a quantity of manacles, and selected the smallest pair he could find, and placed them round her wrists.

Agnes, with a smile, shook her hands, and they fell clanking at her feet.

The prefect then ordered her to death by the sword.

The Roman tradition is that she suffered where is now her church, by the Piazza Navona; but executions were never carried out within the walls of Rome. She was taken to the place where she was to die. Here she knelt, and with her own hands drew forward her hair, so as to expose her neck to the blow. A pause ensued; the executioner was trembling with emotion, and could not brandish his sword.

The interpolated Acts say that before this an angel had brought her a white robe, which she put over her. What is probable is that the magistrate, ashamed of what he had done, suffered one of those angels of mercy, the deaconesses, to reclothe the girl.

As the child knelt in her white robe, with her head inclined, her arms crossed on her breast, and her golden hair hanging to the ground, she must have looked like a beautiful lily, stooping under its weight of blossom.

"And thus, bathed in her rosy blood," says the author of the Acts, "Christ took to Himself His bride and martyr."

Her parents received the body, and carried it to the cemetery they had in their vineyard on the Nomentian Way, and there laid it in a loculus, a recess cut in the side of one of the passages underground. It was probably just under one of the luminaria, or openings to the upper air, which allowed light to enter the Catacombs; for here, two days later, Emerentiana, a catechumen, the foster-sister of Agnes, was found kneeling by her grave; and the pagan rabble, peering in and seeing her, pelted her with stones, stunned, and then buried her under the earth and sand they threw in.

Constantine the Great built the church over the tomb, removing the upper crust; but it was rebuilt by Honorius I., between 625 and 638. It was altered in 1490 by Innocent VIII.; but retains more of the ancient character than most of the Roman churches.

The day on which Agnes suffered was January 21st. The memory of her has never faded from the Church. It is said that her parents dreamed, seven days after her death, that they saw her in light, surrounded by a Virgin band, and with a white lamb at her side. In commemoration of this dream—which not improbably did take place—the Roman Church observes in her honour the 28th of January as well as the actual day of her death.

So ancient is the cult of S. Agnes, that, next to the Evangelists and Apostles, no saint's effigy is older. It appears on the ancient glass vessels used by the Christians in the early part of the century in which she died, with her name inscribed, which leaves no doubt as to her identity.

Mrs. Jameson says of the Church of S. Agnese, in Rome: "Often have I seen the steps of this church, and the church itself, so crowded with kneeling worshippers at Matins and Vespers, that I could not make my way among them; principally the women of the lower orders, with their distaffs and market baskets, who had come thither to pray, through the intercession of the patron saint, for the gifts of meekness and chastity."

In the corrupted Acts, it is told that Agnes was set on a pyre to be burned to death, but that the fire was miraculously extinguished. This is purely apocryphal. It originates in a passage by S. Ambrose, in which he speaks of her hands having been stretched over the fire on a pagan altar, to force her to do sacrifice. This has been magnified into an immense pyre.

"At this age," said he, "a young girl trembles at an angry look from her mother; the prick of a needle draws tears. Yet, fearless under the bloody hands of her executioners, Agnes is immovable under the heavy chains which weigh her down; ignorant of death, but ready to die, she presents her body to the edge of the sword. Dragged against her will to the altar, she holds forth her arms to Christ through the fires of the sacrifice; and her hand forms, even in those flames, the sign which is the trophy of a victorious Saviour. She presents her neck and her two hands to the fetters which they produce for her; but it is impossible to find any small enough to encircle her delicate limbs."

IV

FEBRONIA OF SIBAPTE

The Church had endured a long period of peace after the persecution of Decius, in 250; and in the half-century that had followed, although there had been recrudescences of persecution, it had been spasmodic and local.

During those fifty years the Church had made great way. Conversions had been numerous, persons in high station suffered not only their slaves, but their wives and children, to profess themselves Christians. Places about the court, even in the imperial household, were filled with Christians; and even some were appointed to be governors of provinces, with exemption from being obliged to assist at the usual sacrifices. The Christians built churches of 56their own, and these not by any means small and such as might escape observation.

But, internally, there had been a great development of her own powers in the Church, such as had not been possible when she was proscribed, and could only exercise her vital functions in secret.

And among one of the most remarkable and significant phenomena of this vigorous expansion of life was the initiation of monastic life. In Syria and in Egypt there had for long been something of the kind, but not connected with Christianity.

In Palestine were the Essenes. They numbered about four thousand; they lived in convents, and led a strange life. Five writers of antiquity speak of them—Josephus, Philo, Pliny the Elder, Epiphanius and Hippolytus. They were a Jewish sect, a revolt against Pharisaism, and a survival of the schools of the prophets.

Of fervent and exalted piety, of ardent conviction impatient of the puerilities and the bondage of Rabbinism, they sought to live to God in meditation and prayer and study.

57They built for themselves great houses on the eastern shore of the Dead Sea, which they occupied. They observed the law of Moses with great literalness; they had all things in common; they fasted, prayed, and saw visions. They did not marry, they abstained from wine, they tilled the soil when not engaged in prayer. They were, in a word, monks, but Jewish monks.

When Christianity spread, it entered into and gave a new spirit to these communities without their changing form.

In Egypt, in like manner were the Theraputæ, not Jews, nor confined to Egypt, but most numerous there. They were

20

conspicuous for their habits of great austerity and self-mortification. They left their homes, gave up their substance, fled towns and lived in solitary places, in little habitations or cells apart yet not distant from one another. Each had his little oratory for prayer and praise. They neither ate nor drank till the sun set. Some ate only once in three days, and then only bread, flavoured with salt and hyssop. They prayed twice a day, and between the times 58of prayer read, meditated or worked. Men and women belonged to the order, but lived separately though sometimes praying in common.

Here again we see the shell into which the new life entered, without really changing or greatly modifying the external character.

Doubtless the teaching of the Gospel reached these societies, was accepted, and gradually gave to them a Christian complexion— that was all.

Whether this sort of life was in accordance with the Gospel, was not doubted by them, having before them the example of Christ who retreated into the wilderness for forty days, and His words exhorting to the renunciation of everything that men hold dear, and the recommendation to sell everything, give to the poor, and follow in His footsteps.

It is significant that it was precisely in Palestine where the Essenes had flourished, and in Egypt that the Therapeutæ had maintained such numerous colonies that we find the most vigorous development of monachism. It is not possible to doubt that the one slid into the other imperceptibly.

The persecution of Diocletian broke out in 304. At that time there was at Sibapte, in Syria, a convent of fifty virgins.

One of these, named Febronia, aged eighteen, was the niece of the abbess, Bryene. She was wondrously fair of face and graceful of form, and the old sisters seem to have regarded her with reverence as well as love, because of her marvellous loveliness of body as well as innocence of soul. Apparently when quite young she had lost her parents, and had been taken by her aunt into the convent in earliest infancy, so that she had grown up among the sisters, as a sweet flower, utterly ignorant of the world.

She had studied Scripture so deeply, and was so spiritual in mind, that many ladies living in the cities of Syria came to visit and consult her. Bryene drew a curtain between her niece and those who visited her, so as not to distract her thoughts, as also not to expose her to the gaze of vulgar curiosity.

One day a young heathen woman came to the monastery in the first grief at the loss of her husband, to whom she had been married but seven months. She had found no comfort in the religion of her parents, who could not assure her that the soul had any life

21

after death; it was no true consolation to her to set up a monument in honour of the deceased, and so, hearing of Febronia, she came to Bryene, and falling at her feet, entreated to be allowed to tell her trouble to the girl Febronia.

The abbess hesitated, as the woman was a pagan; but at length, moved by her tears and persistency, gave consent, admitted her into the cell of the nun, and allowed her to tarry with her as long as she pleased.

They passed the night together. Febronia opened the Gospel and read to the broken-hearted woman the words of life. They fell on good ground. The widow wept and listened, and wept again, and as the sun rose on them, she begged to be properly instructed, so as to receive baptism.

When she was gone, "Who," asked Febronia, "was that strange woman who came to me, and who cried as though her heart would break when I read the Scriptures to her?"

"It was Hiera," answered the nun Thomais, who afterwards committed the whole narrative to writing. "Hiera is the widow of a senator."

"Oh," said Febronia, "why did you not inform me of her rank? I have been talking to her just as if she had been my sister."

The noble widow did become the sister of the nun in the faith, and in the family of Christ; and when, some time after, Febronia fell very ill, Hiera insisted on being allowed to be with her and nurse her with her own hands.

Febronia was but convalescent, and looking white as a lily, when Selenus, charged with the execution of the imperial decree against Christians, arrived at Sibapte. He was accompanied by his nephews Lysimachus and Primus, the former of whom was suspected by Diocletian of having a leaning towards Christianity, as his mother had been of the household of faith, and he was a youth of a singularly meditative and temperate life.

Selenus accordingly brought his nephews with him, to associate them with himself in the deeds of cruelty that were meditated, and to awe them into dread of transgressing the will and command of the emperor.

Primus was a cousin on his mother's side to Lysimachus, and he shared with him disgust at the cruelty of their uncle, and they did what was in their power—they sent timely warning to the Christians to escape from a city that was about to be visited.

As soon as the bishop and clergy of Sibapte heard that the governor purposed coming to the place, they dispersed and secreted themselves. The sisters of the convent in great agitation waited on the abbess, and entreated her to allow them to escape for their lives.

Bryene bade them entertain no alarm, as the danger only threatened, and was not at their doors: such humble, insignificant folk as they might expect to be overlooked. At the same time she was really distracted with anxiety, as Febronia was not strong enough to be removed, and she could not leave her.

The sisters took counsel together, and electing one named Aetheria as their spokeswoman, made a second remonstrance, and complained, "We know what is your real reason for retaining us: it is that you are solicitous about Febronia; but the bishop and clergy are in hiding. Do try to carry Febronia away, and suffer us to leave."

Febronia, however, could not be moved, so Bryene dismissed the nuns, and they decamped forthwith; two alone remained— Thomais, the writer of the history, and Procla, who acted as nurse to the sick girl, and who could not find the heart to tear herself away.

Almost immediately after the sisters had fled, news reached those who remained that the governor had arrived. Febronia heard her aunt sobbing. She looked at Thomais, and asked, "I pray you, dear mother, what is the great mistress" (for this was the title of the abbess) "crying so bitterly about?"

"My child," answered the old nun, "she is sore at heart about you. We are old and ugly, and all that can chance to us is death; but you are young and fair, and there are things we fear for you of which you know nothing. We need not say more to you, dearest child, than bid you be very cautious how you accept any offers made to you by the governor, however innocent they may appear. A danger lurks behind them of which you have no conception."

The night passed in anxious conversation and in mutual encouragement. Next morning Selenus sent soldiers to the convent, who broke open the door, and would have cut down Bryene, had not Febronia started from her pallet, and casting herself at their feet, implored them to kill her rather than her old aunt.

Primus arrived at this juncture, rebuked the soldiers for their violence, and bade them go outside the house. Then, turning to Bryene, he asked somewhat impatiently why she had not taken advantage of the warning that had been sent, and escaped.

"Even now," said he, "I will make shift to help you. I will withdraw the soldiers, and do you escape by the back of the house."

Primus then withdrew, and it is possible that the three nuns and Febronia might have escaped, but that Selenus, suspicious of his nephew, sent back the soldiers with peremptory orders to secure Febronia and bring her before him. This was done, and she and the rest were thrown for the night into the common prison.

Next day Selenus ascended the tribunal, and was

23

accompanied by his nephews Primus and Lysimachus, whom he forced to attend.

Bryene and Thomais appeared, each holding a hand of the sick girl and sustaining her. They begged to be tried and condemned with her.

"They are a pair of old hags," said Selenus. "Dismiss them."

Then they were separated from their charge.

"Mother," said Febronia, clinging to and kissing Bryene, "I trust in God that, as I have been ever obedient to thee in the monastery, so I may be faithful to what thou hast exhorted me to do, faithful here openly before all the people. Go then—do not stay here, but pray for me, but before leaving give me thy benediction."

Then she slid to her knees, and Bryene, stretching her hands to heaven, cried: "Lord Jesus Christ, who didst appear to Thy handmaid Thecla, in her agony, to comfort her, stand by Thy lowly one in her great contest."

So saying, she fell on the neck of Febronia, and they kissed and wept and clung to each other till parted by the soldiers.

Then, unable to bear the sight of what she knew must follow, Bryene retired to the deserted convent, and begged that word might be sent her as to how all ended.

In the meantime, Hiera had heard of the arrest of Febronia, and wild with grief she rushed to the place of judgment. She found the court crammed with people, mostly women, agitated, indignant, and murmuring. There was a space clear before the tribunal, where stood the accused, and at one side were various instruments of torture, and a stake driven into the ground furnished with rings and ropes. On the judgment seat were Selenus, with his nephews by him.

Selenus turned to Lysimachus, and said, "Do you open the examination."

The young man, struggling with his emotion, began—"Tell me, young maiden, what is thy condition?"

"I am a servant," answered Febronia.

"Whose servant?" asked Lysimachus.

"I am the servant of Christ."

"And tell me thy name, I pray thee."

"I am a humble Christian," answered Febronia.

"May I ask thy name, maiden?"

"The good mother always calls me Febronia."

Then Selenus broke in: "We shall never have done if you push along in this fashion. To the point at once. Febronia, I vow by the gods that I have no desire to hurt thee. Here is a gallant young gentleman, my nephew; take him as thy husband, and forget the

24

silly stuff, thy religion. I had other views for the boy, but that matters not; never have I seen a sweeter face than thine, and I am content to accept thee as my niece. I am a man of few words: accept my offer, and all is well; or by the living gods I will make thee rue the refusal."

Febronia replied calmly, "I have a heavenly Bridegroom, eternal; with celestial glory as His dower."

Selenus burst forth with, "Soldiers, strip the wench." He was obeyed; they allowed her to wear only a tattered cloak over her shoulders.

68Calm, without a sign of being discomposed, Febronia bore the outrage.

"How now, you impudent hussy?" scoffed Selenus; "where is your maiden modesty? I saw no struggles, no blushes."

"God Almighty knows, judge, that till this day I have never seen the face of man, for I was only two years old when I was taken as a little baby to my aunt, and the rest of my life I have spent there among the good sisters. Do I seem lost to shame? Nay, I have been assured that wrestlers strip in the games when they strive for victory. I fear thee not."

"Stretch her, face downwards, over a slow fire. Bind her hands and feet to four stakes, and so—scourge her."

He was obeyed, and the crimson blood trickled over her white skin at every stroke of the lash, and hissed in the glowing charcoal.

The multitude, looking on, could not bear the sight, and with one voice entreated that she might be removed and dismissed.

But the shouts only made Selenus more angry, and he ordered the executioners to redouble the blows. Thomais, unable to endure the sight, fainted at the feet of Hiera, who uttered a cry of "Oh, Febronia, my sister! Thomais is dying."

The poor sufferer turned her head, and asked the executioner to throw water over the face of the fainting woman, and begged to be allowed to say a word to Hiera.

But the judge interposed to forbid this indulgence, and ordered Febronia to be untied and placed on the rack.

This was sometimes called "the little horse." It had four legs united by planks. At each end was a crank. The sufferer was attached by the feet and hands at ankles and wrists to cords that passed over rollers between the planks. She thus hung below and between the two pieces of wood. At a signal from the magistrate, the executioners turned the cranks, and these drew the feet and hands tighter towards the rollers, and strained them, so that if this were persisted in, the limbs were pulled out of joint.

"Well, girl," asked Selenus, "how do you like your first taste of torture?"

"Learn from the manner in which I have borne it, that my resolution is unalterable," answered Febronia.

On the rack her sides were torn with iron combs. She prayed incessantly: "O Lord, make haste to help me. Leave me not, neither forsake me in my hour of pain!"

"Cut out her tongue," ordered the judge.

Febronia was detached from the rack and tied to the post in the centre of the place. But when the multitude saw what the executioner was about to do, the excitement and indignation became so menacing, that the judge thought it prudent to countermand the order. Instead of which, however, he bade the surgeon in attendance extract her teeth. When he had drawn seventeen, Selenus bade him desist.

"Cut off her breasts."

This atrocious order caused a renewed uproar. The physician hesitated. But Selenus was fairly roused. "Coward, go on! Cut!" he shouted, and the surgeon, with a sweep of the razor, sliced off her right breast.

Febronia uttered a cry as she felt the steel gash her: "My Lord! my God! see what I suffer, and receive my soul into Thy hands."

These were the last words she spoke.

"Cut off the other breast, and put fire to the wound," said Selenus.

He was obeyed. The mob swayed and quivered with indignation; women wept and fainted. Then with a roar broke forth the execration, "Cursed be Diocletian and all his gods!"

Thereupon Hiera sent a girl running to the convent to Bryene to tell her all. And the old abbess flung herself on the ground sobbing, "Bra, bra, bra! Febronia, my child!" Then raising her arms and straining her eyes to heaven, she cried, "Lord, regard Thy humble handmaiden, Febronia, and may my aged eyes see the battle fought out, and my dear child numbered with the martyrs."

In the meantime Selenus had ordered the cords to be removed which bound Febronia to the stake. Then she dropped in a heap on the sand, her long hair flowing over and clothing her mangled body.

Primus said under his breath to his cousin, "The poor girl is dead."

"She died to bring light and conviction to many hearts—perhaps to mine," answered Lysimachus aloud, that his uncle might hear. "Would that it had been in my power to have saved her! Now let her finish her conflict and enter into her rest."

Then Hiera, bursting into the arena, stood wild with

indignation and anguish before the judge, and shrieked, as she shook her hands at him,—"O monster of cruelty! shame on thee, shame! Thou, born of a woman, hast forgotten the obligation to honour womanhood, and hast insulted and outraged thy mother in the person of this poor girl. God, the Judge above judges, will make a swift work with thee, and cut it short, and root thee out of the land of the living."

Selenus, stung with these words, exasperated at the resentment of the mob, and finding that he had fairly roused his nephews into defiance of his authority, shouted his orders to have the widow put on the rack.

But at this point some of the town authorities interfered, and warned the judge that he was proceeding to dangerous lengths. Hiera was well connected, popular; and if she were tortured, a riot was certain to ensue. "Half the town will rush here and insist on being tried and tortured. They will all confess Christ."

Selenus reluctantly gave orders for the release of Hiera, and directed the current of his rage on Febronia, now unconscious. He ordered first her hands, then her feet, and finally her head to be struck off; and when all was finished, rose from his seat, turned to Lysimachus, and saw that his face was bathed in tears. He hastily withdrew to supper, angry with himself, his nephews, and the mob.

Lysimachus and Primus descended to the arena, and standing by the mutilated body, vowed to renounce the gods of Diocletian and to worship the God of Febronia. Then the young men gave orders for the removal of the mangled remains to the house of Bryene.

Almost the whole city crowded to see the body of the young girl who had suffered so heroically.

That night Lysimachus could not eat or speak at supper, and Selenus forced himself to riotous mirth and drunk hard.

We cannot quite trust what follows. It was too tempting to a copyist to allow the governor to go away unchastised. Perhaps it is true that in a drunken and angry fit Selenus, pacing the room storming, slipped on the polished pavement, and in falling hit his head against a pillar—with the result that he never spoke again, having congestion of the brain, and died next day. It is quite possible that this may be true. If it were an interpolation by a copyist, he would have killed him by fire falling from heaven and consuming him—that was the approved way with the re-writers of the Acts of Martyrs.

When Constantine became Emperor both the young men were baptised, retired into solitude and embraced the monastic life.

27

The name of Febronia is in the Greek, Coptic and Abyssinian Kalendars. The simple and apparently quite trustworthy account of her death was by Thomais, the nun who saw her die, and had known her all her short life.

V

THE DAUGHTER OF CONSTANTINE

Constantia, whose name does not appear in the Roman Kalendar, but which has found its way into several unauthorised lists of the Saints, is chiefly known through the Acts of S. Agnes. Little or nothing reliable is recorded concerning her, and her story would not have been included in this collection, were it not for two circumstances—one, that two of the most interesting monuments of Old Rome are associated with her name, one directly, the other indirectly; and next, that a caution, very desirable of being exercised, may be learned from a consideration of her story—not to cast over as utterly fabulous and worthless the legends that come down to us of the Saints of early times, because they are stuffed with unhistorical and ridiculous incidents and marvels. 78Let us now see very briefly what the legend is concerning Constantia.

She was the daughter of Constantine the Great, and was afflicted with a distressing disease, supposed at the time to be leprosy, but which was in all probability scrofula.

The Roman general, Gallicanus, having been in favour with the Emperor, and having lost his wife, was offered Constantia in marriage by his master—not a particularly inviting proposal, and Gallicanus did not, possibly, regret that he was called away by an inroad of the barbarians into Thrace, to defend the Roman frontiers against them. Before engaging in battle he made a vow, in the event of success, that he would believe in Christ and be baptised. He succeeded in repulsing the enemy, and returned to Rome to find that Constantia had been healed of her disorder at the tomb of S. Agnes, and that she had persuaded his three daughters, Augusta, Attica, and Artemia, to live with her, as consecrated virgins, near the shrine of the Virgin Martyr, to whose intercession she attributed her cure.

Constantia had two chamberlains, John and Paul, to whom, at her death, she bequeathed much of her possessions.

When Julian the Apostate assumed the purple, in 361, he did not openly persecute the Church, but he turned out of their situations such officers of the court and army as refused to renounce Christ. John and Paul he particularly disliked, partly because they were zealous Christians, and had had much to do with the conversion of Gallicanus, but also because they had obtained by bequest so much of Constantia's estate, which he desired to draw

29

into the imperial treasury. He sent word that they were to be deprived of their offices, and were to be privately put to death in their own house.

Accordingly, when they had retired to their residence on the Cœlian Hill, the ministers of Julian pursued them, dismissed the servants, and secretly conveyed them down into the cellar of their palace, and there killed and buried them.

Three persons, however, knew of what was going on—Crispinus, Crispinianus, and Benedicta—and, to prevent the matter getting bruited about, these the soldiers also put to death.

Gallicanus was living at Ostia, and he was ordered into exile. He withdrew to Alexandria, where the chief magistrate, Baucianus, summoned him before his tribunal, required him to do sacrifice to idols, and, because he refused, had him decapitated. He has found a place in the Roman Martyrology on June 25th.

Now the whole series of incidents is full of difficulties. The name of Gallicanus was not uncommon. Vulcatius Gallicanus was prefect of Rome in 317, and Ovius Gallicanus was Consul in 330, but of either of them being engaged against the barbarians in Thrace there is no historical evidence.

It is also incredible that the Gallicanus of the legend should have been publicly tried as a Christian and condemned as such under Julian.

The Emperor Constantine had a daughter, Constantia, we know from profane history, who was married to Hannibalianus—a thoroughly unprincipled woman, in fact, if we may trust the highly coloured picture drawn of her by Ammianus Marcellinus. She was a demon in human form, a female fury ever thirsting for blood. But though generally called Constantia, her correct name was Flavia Julia Constantina.

Of the Constantia of the legend there is no mention by the historical writers of the time; but this is not remarkable if she were, as is represented in the story, a woman who took no part in public life, but lived in retirement, partly because of her disorder, and then because she had embraced the religious life.

A further difficulty arises in the account of the martyrdom of SS. John and Paul, her chamberlains. The Acts represent them as subjected to interrogation by Julian himself in Rome, whereas it is quite certain that after he became Emperor he did not set foot in Italy.

It will be seen, therefore, that there is here every reason for repudiating the whole story as fabulous, and some would go so far as to say that Constantia, the virgin daughter of Constantine, Gallicanus, John and Paul were all of them mythical characters, creatures of the imagination. But there are certain very good and weighty reasons on the other side for inducing an arrest of judgment.

In the first place, close to the basilica and catacomb of S. Agnese is a very interesting and precious circular church, erected by Constantine the Great, at the request of his daughter Constantia, as a thankoffering for her recovery from the distressing disease which had disfigured her and made life a burden to her. This church is, perhaps, the most remarkable specimen we have existing of ecclesiastical architecture of the age of Constantine. It is quite untouched, and is rich with frescoes of the period.

But a still more remarkable monument is one quite recently disinterred. It is the house of the martyrs John and Paul, which has existed for centuries buried under the foundations of the great church that bears their names on the Cœlian Hill, a church erected by the one English Pope, Nicolas Breakespeare, in 1158. The discovery of the house is itself a romance. What is known of its early history is this: Julian the Apostate died in 363. The death of John and Paul had taken place in 362. Julian was followed by Jovian, who died in 364, and was succeeded by Valentinian.

Now, directly Julian was no more, Byzantius, a senator and a Christian, interested himself in the matter. The recent martyrdom was in all mouths, and it was known that the bodies lay in the cellar of the house. Byzantius had the bodies lifted and placed in a white alabaster or marble box, and converted the upper storey of the house into an oratory.

The son of Byzantius was Pammachius, the friend and correspondent of S. Jerome. He did something also. He erected a handsome church over the tomb of the saints, and this was completed in 410, forty-eight years after their martyrdom.

There had, however, been no break in the tradition, for Byzantius had made his oratory only two or three years later than their martyrdom.

The basilica erected by Pammachius consisted of an oblong nave, with side aisles and an apse to the west. To the east end was a quadrangle, surrounded by a cloister, and with a water-tank in the middle. By means of a flight of steps visitors were enabled to descend to the "Confession," or place whence they could look down on the alabaster box containing the relics of the martyrs in the cellar; and in the angles of the wall below, a triangular white marble table was placed, hollowed out in the middle for oil, in which a wick burned to throw light on the tomb.

Hard by, in later years, was the family mansion of S. Gregory the Great, who sent Augustine and his little band, in 597, to convert

31

the Anglo-Saxons of Kent. Now, Gregory knew well this church of SS. John and Paul, and often prayed there. Somewhere about 603 he sent a present to Queen Theodelinda, the Bavarian Princess, who had married Agilulph, the Lombard, and among other things some of the oil from this very lamp. This identical vial of oil is preserved among the treasures of Monza, along with some little gold hens and chickens presented by Theodelinda.

Now, a few years ago, Padre Germano, a Passionist father of the monastery attached to the church, in studying the blank south wall of the church that rises out of the little lane, the Clivus Scauri, by which one mounts to reach the entrance of the church, observed that it consisted of a whole series of blocked-up arches and windows above them. In a word, it looked like a three-storey shop-front, or factory of brick, with the openings filled in. What could be the meaning of this? Such an arrangement was not suitable to the basilica of Pammachius, and had certainly no significance for the Church of Adrian I.

Then, all at once, it flashed on him what it really was: it was nothing more nor less than the street-front of the palace of John and Paul, which had been solidly built, and consequently had been utilised first by Pammachius and then by Adrian I. Now the church is built at the top of a steep slope, and the level of the floor of the church is far above the arches. It next occurred to the Padre: Is it not possible that the old house of the martyrs may be beneath the floor of this church?

He obtained leave to search. He went round to persons interested in Christian antiquities, and begged a little money, and so was enabled to begin his excavations; and, lo! he discovered that when in 410 Pammachius had built his basilica he had filled in the lower portion of the house, all the most important rooms and the cellars, with earth and rubbish, and had raised his church above it all, knocking away the floors of the upper storeys and blocking up what had been the bedroom windows. The writer of this account was in Rome during two winters when the Padre was engaged on the excavations, and was frequently there, and saw the results as they were reached. And these results were: first, that a Christian mansion of the fourth century was disinterred, the only one of the kind known to exist; and more, the tomb of the saints into which Byzantius had put the bodies was found; also the very lamp-table from which S. Gregory took the oil for sending to Theodelinda, and the early altar set up by Byzantius in one of the halls of the house which he had converted into an oratory. Nay, more,—paintings were found, whether of the date of Byzantius or of his son Pammachius is uncertain—one representing the soldiers killing Crispinus,

Crispinianus, and Benedicta, and another showing Constantia, with her two chamberlains and other attendants. There were also figures which may be Byzantius and his wife, or Pammachius and his, bringing gifts to the tomb of the martyrs. The cellar was discovered with the old wine-bottles, some marked with the sacred sign; and the frescoes in the reception-room were Christian: a woman lifting up holy hands in prayer; Moses, with the roll of the Law; the good sheep and the bad one, with the Milk of the Word, and so on.

Now, all this shows conclusively that there really were such martyrs as John and Paul, and that although their story has been embroidered, there is a substratum of truth in it.

What is probably the basis of the whole story is this: that Constantia, an infirm, scrofulous daughter of Constantine, residing in Rome, believing herself to have received some alleviation in her condition by praying at the tomb of S. Agnes, not only induced her father to build a basilica above that tomb, but also the remarkable Church of St. Constanza, which is hard by. That she had chamberlains named John and Paul, devout Christians, is also more than probable, as also that she bequeathed to them a large portion of her fortune. The fact of their being zealous Christians, and exerting themselves vigorously to advance the Faith, that among other converts they made was Ovius Gallicanus, who had been Consul in 330, is also probable. That they were secretly put to death in their own mansion on the Cœlian Hill, by the orders of Julian, and buried in their cellar, is quite certain. The chain of evidence is unbroken.

That Constantia had as her friends and fellows in her retired devout life three of the daughters of the ex-Consul, is not at all unlikely. That he was banished to Alexandria by Julian may be admitted. But this is the utmost. The recomposer of the Acts tried to spice the story to suit the taste of his times, and in doing so fell into extravagances, anachronisms, and absurdities.

Constantia may have felt grateful for the disorder that kept her out of the current of public life, and from the intrigues of the palace.

Her father, with all his good qualities, was a violent man; and his adoption of Christianity was due to political shrewdness rather than to conviction.

In 324 Crispus, her accomplished brother, whose virtues and glory had made him a favourite with the people, was accused of conspiring against his father by his stepmother Fausta, who desired to clear him out of the way to make room for her own son Constantius. Another involved in the same charge was Licinius, a son of the sister of Constantine, and who was also a young man of good qualities.

Constantine was at Rome at the time. He went into a fit of blind fury, and had his son put to death, and ordered the execution of Licinius. Then, coming to his senses, and finding that he had acted without having any evidence of the truth of the charges, he turned round on his wife Fausta, and ordered her to be suffocated in a vapour bath.

Constantine died in 337.

"One dark shadow from the great tragedy of his life reached to his last end, and beyond it," says Dean Stanley. "It is said that the Bishop of Nicomedia, to whom the Emperor's will had been confided, alarmed at its contents, immediately placed it for security in the dead man's hand, wrapped in the vestments of death. There it lay till Constantius arrived, and read his father's dying bequest. It was believed to express the Emperor's conviction that he had been poisoned by his brothers and their children, and to call on Constantius to avenge his death. That bequest was obeyed by the massacre of six out of the surviving princes of the imperial family. Two alone escaped. With such a mingling of light and darkness did Constantine close his career."[2]

One of Constantia's sisters, Constantina, has been already mentioned. Her second husband was Gallus. "She was an incarnate fury," says Ammianus Marcellinus; "never weary of inflaming the savage temper of her husband. The pair, in process of time, becoming skilful in inflicting suffering, hired a gang of crafty talebearers, who loaded the innocent with false charges, accusing them of aiming at the royal power or of practising magic." Those accused were all put to death and their goods confiscated. She died of fever in 353.

Another sister, Helena, was married to the Apostate Julian. Her brother, Constantius, although a Christian, was as ensanguined with murders as one of the old Cæsars. Her brothers Constans and Constantine II. fought each other, and Constantine was slain. Violence, bloodshed, stained the whole family, except perhaps Helena and certainly the blameless Constantia. In the midst of such violence and crime, it was indeed something to disappear from the pages of the profane historian and to be remembered only as a builder of churches.

The rotunda near S. Agnese, that bears Constantia's name, was erected during her life, to serve as her mausoleum, and in it she and her sister Helena were laid. She was laid in the beautiful

---

[2] "Lectures on the Eastern Church," 1869, p. 218.

sarcophagus of red porphyry that was in the church. This was carried off by Pope Paul II., who intended to convert it to his own use, and it is now preserved in the Vatican.

The vaulting of the church is covered with mosaic arabesques of flowers and birds referring to a vintage.

VI

THE SISTER OF S. BASIL

It is most rare to be able to obtain a glimpse into the home-life of the ancients. In the first centuries of our era, in the Greek and Roman world, life was so much in public, that there was hardly any domestic life at all; and it was only with Christianity that the quiet, retired and sweet home society constituted itself.

In the midst of flaunting paganism, the first believers were driven indoors, so to speak; they were precluded from much of the amusement that went to fill up the time of the heathen. They could not sit on the benches of the amphitheatre, nor attend at the representations of the theatre. They were largely prevented from being present at banquets given by friends, as these began and ended with libations to the gods, and the benediction of the deities called down on the meats. They were precluded from taking part in civil life, by the oaths and sacrifices associated with every official act.

Thinking, feeling, believing differently from their fellow-citizens, they could not associate with them easily abroad, and were consequently driven to find their society in their own homes.

Perhaps it is only in the writings of S. Basil and his brother S. Gregory of Nyssa that we get anything like a look into the interior of a Christian household in the fourth century. It is therefore, although a quiet picture of an uneventful and unexciting existence, full of interest and charm. S. Basil belonged to a family both noble and wealthy, in Cappadocia, in Asia Minor. His ancestors had occupied public positions either as magistrates or at the imperial court.

His grandmother, Macrina, a native of Neocæsarea, in Pontus, had been brought up by S. Gregory the wonder-worker; and she and her husband, whose name is not recorded, were confessors in the persecution of Diocletian. They fled to the wooded mountain sides, leaving their houses and possessions; and in their places of retreat subsisted mainly on the wild deer, that were so tame that they allowed themselves to be easily snared. They remained in concealment for seven years, and it was not till an edict in favour of the Christians was promulgated, on April 30th, 311, that they ventured to return to Neocæsarea.

Macrina died in Pontus about. Her son Basil inherited the piety of his parents, and he took to wife Æmilia, a woman of great virtue, the daughter of a man who had been put to death after having been deprived of his goods by the Emperor Licinius. She had lost her mother in early youth.

Basil and Æmilia were very wealthy. They owned extensive estates in Pontus, Cappadocia and Lesser Armenia; they had a large family, ten children, of whom the eldest was Macrina, named after her grandmother; S. Basil was the eldest son, then came Naucratius, Gregory, afterwards of Nyssa, and Peter, the youngest, afterwards of Sebaste. We know no more of the four younger girls than that they were well provided for in marriage, and one of them had daughters who became superiors of a monastery in Cæsarea under the direction of their uncle, S. Basil.

Basil the elder, the father, died about 349, shortly after the birth of Peter. Æmilia was now left a widow with a large family to look after, but she was assisted in everything by her eldest daughter, Macrina, who was her inseparable companion.

When Macrina had been born she had been confided to a nurse, but it was remarked that she was almost always in her mother's arms. Æmilia took pains to form the mind of the little girl, and give it a religious direction. She taught her first of all sentences from the Book of Wisdom, then made her commit sundry psalms to memory; so that, as her brother Gregory wrote, the Psalter became to her a companion day and night, and she was for ever singing psalms or reciting them in her heart.

Macrina was a good and patient needlewoman. Not only was the house large, but the brothers and sisters needed attention, and their clothes keeping in order, and Æmilia and her eldest daughter were constantly engaged at their needles, to keep pace with the demands of the family; and as they were always together, one mind was but the reflexion of the other.

What tended to make Macrina a still, stay-at-home girl, was an early love affair. She had been engaged by her father's consent to a high-principled, well-born young man, and the marriage was only deferred because of Macrina's youth. But before this took place he fell ill of fever and was carried off rapidly. After this Basil thought of uniting his daughter to some other suitable person, but Macrina urgently entreated to be allowed to remain with her mother. "My dear husband," she said, "is not dead,—he lives with God. He has gone on a far journey—that is all, and I shall remain faithful to him whilst he is away."

Her father did not press her—indeed, the devotion of Macrina to her mother was so tender and so close that he thought neither could bear to be parted. When he also died, then the union of hearts and interests became closer.

As the children grew up they dispersed, and received their

several inheritances; but they all carried away with them indelibly the stamp impressed on their hearts by their mother and eldest sister; and in the end three of them became bishops and saints. Peter, the youngest, had been most in their hands, but the favourite brother was Naucratius.

As soon as all the birds were out of the nest, then Æmilia felt that there was nothing to retain her in the city, and she pined to be away from its dusty streets and noisy market in the green, sweet country, and in quiet with God.

Accordingly she and Macrina retired to a villa they possessed on the banks of the river Iris, at some little distance from the town of Ibora. This they converted into a sort of monastery. The slaves and other servants, if they chose to unite in the same life, were given freedom and accepted on the footing of sisters, no distinction being made between the members of the little community.

S. Gregory of Nyssa says of this society: "They were all as one in what they ate and drank, as to their furniture and cells, and there was no token that they belonged originally to different ranks in the world. There was no ruffle of temper among them, no petty jealousies, no suspicions, no spite .... all their occupation was in prayer and the singing of psalms, which went on night and day."

Peter, the youngest, who had been ordained, lived near at hand, and for the care he had received as a child returned his ministerial offices. S. Basil also for awhile lived in retirement not far off, and was a help and comfort to them.

Macrina suffered about this time from a painful abscess in her breast, and Æmilia constantly urged her to let a doctor examine and lance it. She was afraid lest, should it not be opened, it might break internally. But Macrina was so modest and sensitive—perhaps absurdly so—that she shrank from the ordeal of letting a man treat the place. At last the old lady insisted; the abscess had become so hot and swollen that she was alarmed.

Macrina, struggling against shame, went into the little oratory, and remained weeping and praying there all night, sometimes with her face against the ground and her tears running over the dust. The heat and pain in her breast and the tension were so insupportable, that she gathered up some of the cool earth and pressed it to the swelling, when it burst, and she was relieved; and so the need for calling in a surgeon was overpassed.

At length Æmilia died, at an advanced age. None of her children were with her at the time except Macrina and Peter; however, as she was dying, the old and saintly woman murmured blessings on the absent darlings, and taking Peter by one hand and Macrina by the other, said, "Lord, I offer to Thee my firstfruits and my tithe. Accept them, O Lord, and pour the floods of Thy grace into both their hearts." They were her last words. She died in 373, and was laid beside her husband whom she had loved so well. The grief of Macrina was not to be expressed. She had been the inseparable companion of her mother since her earliest infancy, and they had not had a thought or wish but what was in common.

Before Macrina had recovered from this blow she was called on to endure another. Her favourite brother, Naucratius, was found dead in the field along with his servant Chrysapius, without it being known what had caused their death.

Six years later she was called to mourn the loss of her eldest brother, S. Basil. It was she who, with his friend Gregory Nazianzen, had been the means of turning his heart entirely to God. As a young man he had been disposed to push his way as a statesman. In 355 Basil had been at school with Julian, afterwards Emperor, and an apostate from the faith, and with Gregory, who was the son of the Bishop of Nazianzus. Basil had not formed a high opinion of the former, but with Gregory "it was one soul in two bodies." On returning to Cæsarea after his father's death, Basil turned towards a life in the world, and a prospect of advancement in official life opened to him. It was then that Macrina had exerted all her influence over him, and gave him that final direction which made of him so glorious a saint and teacher of the Church.

And now Macrina had lost him.

In the month of September or October in the year following the death of S. Basil, Gregory—now Bishop of Nyssa—was present at the Council held at Antioch, and on leaving it he resolved on paying a visit to Macrina. He had not seen her since the death of their brother Basil, and he wished to talk with her about him. The journey was long, and the snows were already powdering the lower ranges of the lofty mountains he had to pass.

On the night previous to his arrival on the banks of the Iris, after a tedious and long day's travel, he had a dream. It seemed to him that he held relics in his hands that emitted a blaze of white light.

When he awoke he wondered what this dream could signify, for he was not above the superstition of his age which attributed importance to dreams; but as he neared the monastery he met a servant who told him that Macrina was dangerously ill, and Gregory at once concluded that his dream was a portent of her approaching dissolution.

Sick at heart, he pressed forward, and arrived at the villa. Those within came forth to welcome him, except the sisters, who remained in the church, sorrowful at the prospect of losing their best friend, yet glad that she should see her brother before her death.

Gregory at once entered the church and prayed, and gave his episcopal benediction to all. Then he asked to be conducted to Macrina.

We have an account of the last scene from his own pen, and this shall be given with only a little condensation.

"A woman who was there opened the door to me, and led me within. I found my sister lying on the ground, on a plank covered with sackcloth (the Cilician material made of goat's hair, much in use for blankets) and with a pillow of the same supporting her head. She was very ill, but when she saw me, unable on account of her great weakness to rise and meet me, she lifted herself on one elbow, placing the other hand on the ground for her support. I ran to her, and insisted on laying her down again as she had been. Then she lifted her hands to Heaven and said, 'I thank Thee, O Lord my God, in that Thou hast fulfilled the desire of my heart.'

"She did her utmost to conceal from us what a difficulty she found in breathing, so as not to increase our distress; and her face was bright and smiling, and she spoke of such matters as she thought pleasing to us. But when we came to mention Basil, then my face expressed the grief I was in at his loss. But she, on the contrary, spoke of the matter with serenity of soul and elevation of mind, so that I felt myself as though carried up above all worldly considerations into heavenly regions with her.

"Presently she said, 'Brother, you have had a tedious journey, and must be very tired: I pray you take a little rest.' And although it was a delight to me to listen to her, yet I obeyed; and I went forth into the garden, where was a pleasant shady walk. However, I was in such trouble of mind that I could admire nothing, and I could think only of what must shortly happen.

"I suppose she must have divined my thoughts, for she sent word to me not to fret, as she hoped speedily to be better; but she really meant that she would escape from her present pains, and be with God, for whom her soul ever thirsted. I got up when I heard this, and went to see her again. Then, when we were together, she began to talk about old times, since our childhood, and all as calmly and consequently as though she were reading out of a book. She talked of the mercies shown by God to our father, mother, and all the family.

"I wanted to tell her about my troubles when the Emperor Valens banished me for the Faith, and of other troubles in which I had been involved; but she cut me short with 'Never lose sight of the obligations you owe to God. Think chiefly of the advantages you have received from Him.'

"As she was speaking we heard the song of the virgins calling to vespers, and my sister bade me go to the church. Thus passed the night, and when day dawned I could see clearly by her condition that it would be her last, for the fever had exhausted her last powers.

"My soul was agitated by double feelings: one was grief, for nature would make me feel, and I knew that the words I heard were the last that would be uttered by one very dear to me; the other was admiration at the calm and trust with which she awaited death.

"The sun was nigh setting without her having lost the force of her mind. Then she ceased to speak to us, but folded her hands and fixed her eyes on her heavenly Bridegroom. Her little bed was turned with the feet to the east, and she spoke to Him in a low voice, which we could hardly hear. We did, however, collect some of her words: 'O Lord, Thou deliverest us from the fear of death; Thou makest the close of life the commencement of a new and truer life. Thou sufferest us to sleep awhile, and then wilt call us with the trumpet at the end of time. To the earth Thou entrustest the dust of which Thy hands have fashioned us, to reclaim it and clothe it with immortality and glory. Lord, Thou who on the Cross didst pardon the malefactor, remember me in Thy kingdom.'

"Then Macrina made the sign of the cross on her eyes, her mouth, and her heart; and, the strength of the fever having parched her tongue, we could no longer follow her, but saw that her lips continued to move. She closed her eyes; but when a lamp was brought into the room she opened them, and made a sign that she desired to recite vespers. But her tongue failed her, only her spirit was active, and her lips and hands moved as before, and we understood when she had finished, by her again signing herself.

"Finally she drew a long, deep sigh, and passed away in prayer. Seeing what had taken place, and remembering a wish she had expressed to me, in our last conversation, that I should render her the last offices, I put out my shaking hand to her face to close the eyes and mouth. But I did this only to fulfil my promise, for really there was no need, as eyes and mouth were closed, so that she appeared rather to be sleeping than dead. Her hands lay on her breast, and her body rested modestly, as that of a virgin."

When Macrina was being prepared for burial, there was no other raiment of hers found save her veil, her mantle, habit, and a pair of worn-out shoes. Then Gregory gave one of his own tunics for clothing his sister's body, and over her was cast her mother's black

41

cloak; "and," says Gregory, "the blackness of this cloak made her face seem so much the whiter, as though it shone with light."

As she was being clothed, a widow, who loved her and attended to these last offices, untied a slender string that was round her neck, and released a little cross and an iron ring.

"Keep the cross," said Gregory to the widow, "as a remembrance of her; and I shall ever preserve the ring."

Who can tell? Perhaps that poor little iron ring was the reminiscence of her engagement to the young man to whom she had long ago been betrothed, and to whom she had remained ever faithful.

VII

GENEVIÈVE OF PARIS

S. Geneviève was born and lived in a time of frightful disaster, unparalleled in the history of Europe. From the commencement of the fifth century a veritable deluge of diverse nations, driven on one by another, inundated the crumbling empire, and gave the signal for its complete ruin.

The Franks, under the long-haired Clodion, traversing the forest of the Ardennes, and rolling to the banks of the Somme, had seized on Amiens, Cambrai, Tournai, after having burnt Trèves, and sacked Cologne. The citizens, of Trèves, which had been the residence of emperors since Maximian, had been slaughtered in the circus to which they had fled. The amphitheatre, which under Constantine has streamed with the blood of the Barbarians, was now heaped with the bodies of Romans. Cologne had been revelling in drunken orgy, when a slave ran to announce that the Franks were on the walls. The citizens had not the manhood to rise from table so as to die standing. Their blood mingled with the wine of their overturned cups. God chastised Roman vices with disgrace as with iron. In this fifth century three societies stood face to face—the Old Roman polity, the Barbarian, and the Church. Rome went to pieces under the blows of the Barbarians, but the Barbarian in turn was subjugated by Christianity.

S. Geneviève was born at Nanterre, about seven miles from Paris, in 422 or 423. The old name of the place, Nemetdoor, is purely Celtic, as is her name, which is the same as Gwenever or Gwenhwyvar in Welsh. Her father was named Severus, and her mother Gerontia, the female form of Geraint. There can be no doubt whatever that she was of Gallic origin, but Latinised, and a Christian.

One word, before proceeding, about the authority for her life. This is a biography, written eighteen years after her death, by the priest Genes, her spiritual director. He learned from the saint the general outline of the incidents in her childhood, and these he dressed up in what he believed to be literary style.

Late in the Middle Ages it was said that S. Geneviève had kept sheep for her father, and she is now generally represented as a shepherdess; but there is no early authority for this, although the fact is very probable. In the year 429 S. Germain, Bishop of Auxerre, and S. Lupus, Bishop of Troyes, at the entreaty of the British

43

Church, commissioned for the work by a Council of Gallican bishops, left their dioceses to visit our island, there to withstand the Pelagian heresy, which was making way.

S. Germain was well qualified to go to Britain, as he was of Celtic origin, and his sister was the wife of Aldor, brother of Constantine I., King of Devon and Cornwall.

On his way to the coast he passed through Nanterre. The people, hearing of his approach, lined the road, and with them were the children in goodly numbers.

As Germain and Lupus advanced, the eye of the former rested on a fair little girl of seven, whose devout look, and sweet, innocent face, arrested him. He stood still, and called her to him, then stooped and kissed her on the brow, and asked her name. He was told that she was called Geneviève. The pleased parents now stepped up, and the venerable bishop asked, "Is this your child?"

They answered in the affirmative.

"Then," said Germain, "happy are ye in having a child so blessed. She will be great before God; and, moved by her example, many will decline from evil and incline to that which is good, and will obtain remission of their sins, and the reward of life from Christ." And then, after a pause, he said to the young girl, "My daughter, Geneviève." She answered, "Thy little maiden listens."

Then he said, "Do not fear to tell me whether it be not your desire to devote yourself body and soul to Christ."

She answered, "Blessed be thou, father, for thou hast spoken my desire. I pray God earnestly that He will grant it me."

"Have confidence, my daughter," said Germain; "be of good courage, and what you believe in your heart and confess with your lips, that take care to perform. God will add to your comeliness both virtue and strength."

Then they went into the church and sang nones and vespers, and throughout the office Bishop Germain rested his right hand on the fair little head of the child.

That evening, after supper had been eaten and they had sung a hymn, Germain bade Severus retire with his daughter, but bring her to him again early next morning. So when day broke, Severus returned with the child, and the old bishop smiled, and said, "Welcome, little daughter Geneviève. Do you recollect what was said yesterday?"

She answered, "My father, I remember what I promised, and with God's help what I promised that I will perform."

Then S. Germain picked up a brass coin from the ground, which had the sign of the cross on it, and which he had noticed lying there whilst he was speaking; and he gave it to her, saying, "Bore a hole in this, and wear it round thy neck in remembrance of me, and let no other ornament, or gold or silver or pearls, adorn thy neck and thy fingers." Then he bade her farewell, commending her to the care of her father, and pursued his journey.

Now, we may ask, How much of this is true? Almost everything. Geneviève was certain never to forget how the old bishop had stopped her, when a little mite of seven, how he had asked her name, had made her promise to love and fear God; how in church his hand had rested all through the service on her head, and how he had given her the coin to wear. But as to the prophecy relative to her future, and to his exacting of her a promise to be a nun, all that may be the make-up of Genes, writing after she had been a blessing to the people of Paris, and had embraced the monastic life.

At the age of fifteen she and two other girls somewhat older than herself presented themselves before the bishop to be veiled as dedicated virgins. It was remarked that, although Geneviève was the youngest, yet the bishop consecrated her first.

After their dedication they returned to their homes; for, at that time, it was not a matter of course that consecrated virgins should live in community.

About this time her mother suffered from inflamed eyes, and for twenty-one months, or nearly two years, could not see to do her household work. Accordingly, Geneviève was of immense assistance to her. She was wont repeatedly to bathe her mother's eyes with water from the well, and this in time reduced the inflammation, so that eventually Gerontia recovered her sight.

At last Geneviève lost both her parents, and now, having no home duties to restrain her, she went to Paris into a religious community.

In 447 S. Germain again visited Britain about the same trouble which had occasioned his first journey; and when, on his way, he came to Paris, he inquired for the little girl whom he had blessed at Nanterre eighteen years before.

Genes tells us that some spiteful people sought to disparage her; but Germain would not hearken to them, and sent for and communed with her.

What caused them to make light of her was probably this. She had adopted a life of great asceticism, eating nothing but barley bread and beans, and that only twice in the week; and remaining within her cell, conversing with none from Epiphany till Easter.

There were a number of people in Paris who did not like these extravagances; and it was these, in all probability, who spoke against her to S. Germain. But, as we shall see presently, by this

45

means she did acquire an enormous power over the people of Paris, which she used for good.

S. Germain had probably but just returned from Britain before a new and terrible scourge broke upon Gaul.

In 451, the Huns, headed by their king, Attila, burst in. In two columns this vast horde had ascended the Danube. One of these drew several German peoples along with it, eager for plunder, whilst the other fell on and crushed the isolated Roman stations. This agglomeration of invaders met at the sources of the Danube, crossed the Rhine at Basle, where the proximity to the Black Forest favoured the construction of rafts for passing over.

The Franks, who occupied the right bank of the Rhine, extended their hands to the Huns. The Burgundians, however, offered a vain resistance, and were cut to pieces. The Huns, entering Gaul, completed the destruction of what had been left standing by Vandals, Suevi, and Alans. Attila, following the Rhine as he had the Danube, devastated Alsace. Strasburg, Spires, Worms, ruined by preceding invasions, had not risen from the dust. Mayence was sacked, Toul sank in flames, Metz had its walls and towers overthrown after a few months' resistance. The savage conquerors massacred all, even to the children at the breast. They fired the town, and long after its site could only be recognised by the Chapel of S. Stephen, which had escaped the conflagration.

Several cities opened their gates to Attila: they hoped to find safety in submission; they did but expedite their destruction. Despair gave courage to others, but no heroism availed against these devouring hordes. Rheims and Arras were delivered over to the sack. The host broke up into fractions, which ravaged the country, carrying everywhere fire and sword.

Attila advanced to the Loire.

Then it was that a panic fell on the inhabitants of Paris. In madness of fear, they prepared to desert it: the rich in their chariots and waggons, the poor on foot.

It was now that S. Geneviève stood forward and rebuked their cowardice. Whither could they fly? The enemy penetrated everywhere. The Hun gained audacity by the universal panic. Better man their walls, brace their hearts, and resist heroically.

The Parisian mob, headlong and cruel, as such a mob has ever been, howled at her, and prepared to pelt her with stones and cast her into the Seine, when, opportunely, appeared the Archdeacon of Auxerre, sent expressly to Geneviève from the bishop, just returned from Britain, and now dying, bearing Blessed Bread to her, that he had sent in token of affectionate communion. This loaf, the eulogia, was that from which the bread for the Communion had been taken, and which remained over. It had been blessed, but not consecrated; and it was sent by bishops to those whom they held in esteem.

Such a token of regard paid to Geneviève by one so highly esteemed awed the rabble, and they swung from one temper to another. They were now amenable to her advice. They closed the gates, accumulated the munitions of war, and made preparations to stand a siege; but Attila did not approach. He foresaw that it would take him too long to reduce so strong a place. On the 14th of June, 451, the Huns encountered their first repulse. They were driven from the siege of Orleans. On the field of Châlons-sur-Marne, the memorable battle was fought between Aetius, the Roman general, and Attila. "It was a battle," says the historian Jornandes, "which for atrocity, multitude, horror, and stubbornness has not had its like." The field was heaped with the dead, but it resulted in the expulsion of the Huns from Gaul.

Feeling a great reverence for S. Denis, Geneviève desired greatly to build a church on the scene of his martyrdom; and she urged some priests to undertake the work. But they hesitated, saying that they had no means of burning lime—it was a lost art. Then, so runs the tale, one of them suddenly recollected having heard two swineherds in conversation on the bridge over the Seine. One had said to the other: "Whilst I was following one of my pigs the other day, I lit in the forest on an ancient abandoned lime-kiln."

"That is no marvel," answered the other, "for I found a sapling in the forest uprooted by the wind, and under its roots was an old kiln."

The priests inquired where these kilns were and used them, and Geneviève set the priest Genes, who was afterwards her biographer, to superintend the work of building the church.

It shows to what a condition of degradation the art of building had fallen, when the Parisians were unable to burn lime without old Roman kilns for the purpose.

A little incident, very simple and natural, was afterwards worked up into a marvel. She was going one night from her lodging to the church for prayers, carrying a lantern, when the wind, which was violent, extinguished it. She opened the lantern, when a puff of wind on the thick red glowing wick rekindled the flame. This was thought quite miraculous. It is a thing that has happened over and over again with tallow candles when the snuff is long.

In the year 486, Childeric, King of the Franks, laid siege to Paris, which had remained under Roman governors. The siege lasted ten years, to 496. It cannot have been prosecuted with much persistence.

The Frank army reduced the city to great straits, and famine set in. The poor suffered the extremity of want, and were dying like flies. No one seemed to know what to do. All energy and resourcefulness had deserted those in authority. Geneviève alone showed what steps should be taken: she got into a ship, and was rowed up the Seine, and then up the Aube to Arçis, where she knew that she could obtain corn. In the Seine was a fallen tree with a snag that had been the cause of the loss of several vessels, but no one had thought of removing the obstruction. Geneviève made her boatmen saw up the tree and break it, so that it floated down stream and could effect no further mischief. Another instance of the condition of helplessness into which the debased provincials of Gaul had fallen: they neither could build lime-kilns nor keep their rivers open for traffic. She got together what provisions she could at Arçis, then went on upon the same quest to Troyes, and finally laded eleven barges with corn, and returned with them to the famished city. As they neared Paris a strong gale was blowing, and the barges being laden very heavily ran some risk, especially as here also there were snags in the water. But with patience and trouble they were manœuvred through these impediments, and the convoy arrived in Paris, with the priests singing, and all who were in the boats joining, "The Lord is our help and our salvation. The Lord hath delivered us in the time of trouble."

The joy and gratitude of the Parisians knew no bounds. Afterwards, when the city did fall, Childeric resolved on executing a great host of captives; but Geneviève, in a paroxysm of compassion, rushed to him, fell on her knees, and would not desist from intercession on their behalf till he had consented to spare them.

At length, worn out by age, she died in 512, and was buried in Paris, where now stands the Panthéon. The church was desecrated at the Revolution, and turned into a burial-place for Mirabeau, the regicide Lepelletier de Saint-Fargeau, the brutal Marat, Dampierre, Fabre, Bayle, and other revolutionaries. The bodies of Voltaire and Rousseau were also transferred to it.

In 1806 it was again restored as a church, but was once more turned into a temple after the July revolution of 1830. Once again consecrated in 1851, it was finally secularised in 1885 for the obseq

VIII

THE SISTER OF S. BENEDICT

It looked to the eyes of Christians of the Roman Empire crumbling to pieces as though the end of all things were at hand. From every quarter barbarism was extending over the confines of the Empire and was breaking them down. The civilisation which had been built up through centuries, the organism of political unity, the literature and learning of two great and gifted races, the Greek and the Latin, achievements of art never to be surpassed, and Christianity, all seemed destined to go down and be trodden under foot never to reappear.

Throughout the Church there rose the wail to God—"Thine adversaries roar in the midst of Thy congregations: and set up their banners for tokens. He that hewed timber afore out of the thick trees was known to bring it to an excellent work. But now they break down all the carved work thereof with axes and hammers. They have set fire upon Thy holy places: and have defiled the dwelling-place of Thy Name, even unto the ground. Yea, they said in their hearts, Let us make havock of them altogether: thus have they burnt up all the houses of God in the land. We see not our tokens, there is not one prophet more: no, not one is there among us, that understandeth any more. O God, how long shall the adversary do this dishonour: how long shall the enemy blaspheme Thy Name, for ever?"

Confusion, corruption, despair and death, were everywhere; social dismemberment was complete. The empire that had embraced the known world was crumbling to dust under the blows of the mysterious multitudes passing out of the darkness beyond the pale. Odoacer, the chief of the Heruli, had snatched the purple of the Cæsars from the shoulders of their last representative in 476, but himself disdained to wear a mantle that was stained with cowardice and dishonour. Authority, morals, laws, science, the arts, religion itself, all seemed to be sinking into the vortex of death.

Germany was wholly pagan, a breeding-place of hordes that burst forth periodically to devastate the land that had been cultivated, and to extinguish the light wherever it burned. Gaul had been overwhelmed by successive waves of barbarism. Spain was ravaged by Visigoths, Suevi, Alani, and Vandals. These latter had swept over Northern Africa, and had given it up to unpitying persecution. Britain had been invaded by the Anglo-Saxons, who

49

had driven the Britons and their Christianity to the mountains of Strathclyde, Wales, and to the peninsula of Cornwall. Over the frozen Danube, the Goths had passed on their cumbrous waggons, and had spread from the woody shores of Dalmatia to the walls of Constantinople.

The condition of Italy, the heart and soul of the Empire that had been dissolved, was deplorable to the last degree. For centuries agriculture had decayed in it, as the farms were absorbed by the great senatorial families and worked by their slaves. The people had come to expect their grain from Egypt and Africa, and now these tributary harvests were withdrawn. War, famine, pestilence stalked over its fair plains, and mowed down such as remained of the population. Pope Gelasius affirmed, with some exaggeration, that in Æmilia, Tuscany and the adjacent provinces, the human species was almost extirpated. "The plebeians of Rome," says Gibbon, "who were fed by the hand of their master, perished or disappeared, as soon as his liberality was suppressed; the decline of the arts reduced the industrious mechanic to idleness and want; and the senators, who might support with patience the ruin of their country, bewailed their private loss of wealth and luxury. One-third of those ample estates, to which the ruin of Italy is originally imputed, was extorted for the use of the conquerors. Injuries were aggravated by insults; the sense of actual sufferings was embittered by the fear of more dreadful evils; and as new lands were allotted to new swarms of barbarians, each senator was apprehensive lest the arbitrary surveyors should approach his favourite villa, or his most profitable farm. The least unfortunate were those who submitted without a murmur to the power which it was impossible to resist."

The general despair produced in religious minds the conviction that the fashion of the world was passing away, there was nothing further to be hoped for in it, and that the only direction in which the eternal spring of hope could flow was in the channels of religion that led to heaven.

This was the condition of affairs in Italy, and this explains the origin and the enormous expansion of the Benedictine Order.

S. Benedict was born along with his sister Scholastica in the year 480. They were twins, and loved each other with that tenderness which so generally exists between twins; they were of one heart and one soul.

They belonged to the noble Anician family, whose history is traceable to the second century before Christ.

Benedict and his twin sister were born at Nursia, a Sabine town, situated high up in the mountains near the source of the Nar. It was here that Vespasia Polla, mother of the Emperor Vespasian, was also born. Virgil speaks of the coldness of its climate, as the chilly cradle of the waters of Tiber and Febaris. To the east tower up the Apennines to the peak of the Monte della Sibilla. Two centuries after the death of Benedict, the vast ruins of his ancestral palace were still to be seen outside the town gates.

Doubtless it was to this Alpine retreat that the family had fled to hide themselves from the Gothic invaders who were devouring the land. Benedict and his twin sister, as their minds opened, became aware of the universal hopelessness that possessed men's minds. The doom of the great nobles was as certainly sealed as at the French Revolution. No prospect was open to them of any work, any career in political life. They could not fly the fatherland to the colonies, for the colonies were in the throes as well.

These little children, wandering hand in hand through the empty halls of the palace, became prematurely grave, and at an early age were convinced that the only life open to them was that of religion.

Scholastica was the first to speak out what she felt, and to resolve to devote herself wholly to God. Who could think of marriage then, when there was no prospect of being able to rear a family in sufficiency and to any career? Benedict followed. Leaving his old nurse, to whom the charge of the children had been committed, and who loved them as her own soul, he plunged into the gorges of the mountains to seek for a retreat where he might discipline his body and soul. The place he found was Subiaco, twenty-six miles from Tivoli, up the valley of the Anio. Why he chose this spot we do not know. He can hardly have stumbled on it in his wanderings about Nursia, and it is probable that he went thence from some other villa and estate of his parents.

The first place where he lodged was Mentorella, and there his nurse, Cyrilla, came up with him, and insisted on furnishing him with supplies of food. But thence he soon went on to Subiaco, where he found a cave in the face of the rocks above the falls of the Anio, and there he spent three years. Every day, Romanus, a monk who dwelt amid a colony of anchorites among the ruins of Nero's palace, near at hand, let down to him half a loaf from the top of the rock above, giving him notice of its approach by the ringing of a bell suspended to the same rope with the food.

It was an astounding mode of life for a boy growing into manhood, and we should now consider it a most unprofitable one. But it was not destined to be unprofitable—very much the contrary; and we must remember that there was absolutely no other field for the activities of a young noble open before him.

"How perfectly," says Dean Milman, "the whole atmosphere

was then impregnated with an inexhaustible yearning for the supernatural, appears from the ardour with which the monastic passions were indulged at the earliest age. Children were nursed and trained to expect at every instant more than human interferences; their young energies had ever before them examples of asceticism, to which it was the glory, the true felicity of life, to aspire. The thoughtful child had all his mind thus preoccupied. He was early, it might almost seem intuitively, trained to this course of life; wherever there was gentleness, modesty, the timidity of young passion, repugnance to vice, an imaginative temperament, a consciousness of unfitness to wrestle with the rough realities of life, the way lay invitingly open—the difficult, it is true, and painful, but direct and unerring way to heaven."

Such a life is not needed now-a-days. What is now required is one like that of Angela, in Sir Walter Besant's "All Sorts and Conditions of Men," who will plunge into the sordid wretchedness of the slums of our great cities, and labour there to bring happiness to the dull lives of the toilers—who will labour to ameliorate the condition of those that are the slaves of our nineteenth-century civilisation. What we require—what God requires—are social reformers, men and women, who in place of living selfish lives of amusement and luxury, will devote themselves to helping to raise those who are down, who will seek happiness, not in pampering self, but in making others happy.

After a while crowds of disciples flocked to Benedict, and then he left Subiaco for Monte Cassino, which was thenceforth to be the capital of monastic life.

Strange it may appear, but it was true, that Benedict found the people round Cassino still pagans, offering sacrifices in a temple to Apollo on the height where he chose to plant his settlement.

> "In old days,
> That mountain, at whose side Cassino rests,
> Was, on its height, frequented by a race
> Deceived and ill-disposed; and I it was,
> Who thither carried first the name of Him,
> Who brought the soul-subliming truth to man,
> And such a speeding grace shone over me,
> That from their impious worship I reclaim'd
> The dwellers round about."—*Dante, Par. xxii.*

The visitor to Monte Cassino now leaves the station at San Germano, and hires donkeys for the ascent. The steep and stony path winds above the roofs of the houses of the town, and at every path opens fresh views of entrancing beauty. The silver thread of the Garigliano lies below, with towns studded on its banks; long ranges of mountains of the most beautiful outline break the horizon, billow after billow of intensest blue, crested as with a foam of snow. Little oratories by the wayside commemorate incidents in the life of S. Benedict. First comes that of S. Placidus, the favourite disciple of the patriarch; then that of Scholastica his sister; then one where he is supposed to have wrought a miracle; next a cross on a platform that indicates the place where brother and sister met for the last time—of which more anon. Then a grating and a cross where S. Benedict knelt to ask God's blessing before he laid the foundation stone of his monastery. Benedict had been thirty-six years a monk before he came to Monte Cassino, and we know nothing of his sister's life through all these years, save that she had maintained a still and holy converse with God. It is most probable that she had never tarried very far from her brother. Now that he settled at Monte Cassino, she came and planted herself with a little community of pious women at the foot of the mountain. Scholastica was as white in soul, as earnest, as devout as was Benedict. They were alike in everything save in sex; and she became, as unawares as himself, a mighty foundress—for if from him houses for men multiplied throughout the Western world, so was she the mother spiritual of innumerable similar refuges for holy women.

At Monte Cassino, according to the expression of Pope Urban II., "the monastic life flowed from the heart of Benedict as from the fountain of Paradise," and here it was that he composed his famous rule, that commenced with the words, "Hearken, O my sons" (Ausculta o fili).

When he drew it up, not a notion came into his head that he was doing a work that would last, a work that was absolutely needed for the times, and without which the barbarians would never have been tamed and regenerated, and a new civilisation superior to the old rise out of the ashes of that which expired.

It is quite true that there were plenty of monks and nuns already scattered about; but they were under no definite rule, under no strict obedience. We see exactly how it was among the Celtic societies. An abbot or abbess rambled over the West, now in Ireland, then in Scotland, in Britain, in Armorica, dived into the Swiss gorges, strayed about in the woods of Germany, founding houses and churches, then going farther. And just as the abbots were ever on the move, so was it with those who placed themselves under their teaching. No sooner did they think they knew enough, or no sooner did the itch of change affect them, than away they went, now to pay a brief visit to some other great master, then to be off again and found monasteries of their own. There was no stability about them, and above all no organisation. The idea of obedience never seems to have entered their heads, and, as a matter of course, a great number of vagabonds too idle to work, and loving change, assumed the tonsure and habit, and roved over the country leading scandalous lives; in fact, the Hooligans of the day postured as saints. Monachism, which should have served a high missionary purpose, for lack of organisation was becoming a discredit to Christianity.

There is a striking French tale, "Mon oncle Celestin," by Ferdinand Faber, in which he describes the "ermites" of the Cevennes and the south of France, a set of men who pretend to lead exalted lives, wear a religious habit, are under no ecclesiastical discipline, and who—with some notable exceptions—are a scandal and source of demoralisation. Now the monks and ascetics before S. Benedict were very much like these modern "ermites" of the Cevennes.

The great work of S. Benedict was to coordinate all these ardent men in one body, to subject them to discipline, to insist on obedience, and then to employ their powers for the good of the Church and of humanity in general.

At that period, when nations had to be conquered, and those nations barbarian, the ordinary methods of propagating the faith did not suffice. Single priests were pretty sure to be butchered, or if not, alone they could effect very little. Besides, the barbarians had to be taught something more than Christianity; they had to be instructed in the industrial arts and in agriculture.

Now, the Benedictine monastery was not only a missionary establishment containing a great many men, but it was a school, a hospital, a poorhouse, a great workshop, and an agricultural institution.

But we must leave this interesting topic to speak of S. Scholastica.

As already said, she had established herself at the foot of the mountain with a community of like-minded women who were under the direction of her brother. They met only once a year; and then it was that Scholastica left her cloister to seek Benedict. He, on his side, descended part way to meet her; and the place where they clasped hands and looked into each other's eyes was on the mountain side, not very far from the gate of the monastery.

"There, at their last meeting, occurred that struggle of fraternal love with the austerity of the rule, which is the only episode in the life of Scholastica, and which has insured an imperishable remembrance to her name. They had passed the entire

54

day in pious conversation, mingled with the praises of God. Towards evening they ate together.

"While they were still at table, and the night approached, Scholastica said to her brother, 'I pray thee do not leave me to-night, but let us speak of the joys of heaven till the morning.' 'What sayest thou, my sister!' answered Benedict; 'on no account can I remain out of the monastery.'

"Upon the refusal of her brother, Scholastica bent her head between her clasped hands on the table, and prayed to God, shedding tears to such an extent that they ran over the table. The weather was at the time serene: there was not a cloud in the sky. But scarcely had she raised her head, when thunder was heard muttering, and a storm began. The rain, lightning, and thunder were such, that neither Benedict nor any of the brethren who accompanied him could take a step beyond the roof that sheltered them.

"Then he said to Scholastica, 'May God pardon thee, my sister, but what hast thou done?' 'Ah yes!' she answered him, 'I prayed thee, and thou wouldst not listen to me; then I prayed God, and He heard me. Go now, if thou canst, and send me away, to return to my convent.'

"He resigned himself, against his will, to remain, and they passed the rest of the night in spiritual conversation. S. Gregory, who has preserved this tale to us, adds that it is not to be wondered at God granting the desire of the sister rather than that of the brother, because of the two it was the sister who loved most, and that those who love most have the greatest power with God.

"In the morning they parted, to see each other no more in this life. Three days after, Benedict, being at the window of his cell, had a vision, in which he saw his sister entering heaven under the form of a dove. Overpowered with joy, his gratitude burst forth in songs and hymns to the glory of God. He immediately sent for the body of the saint, which was brought to Monte Cassino, and placed in the sepulchre he had already prepared for himself, that death might not separate those whose souls had always been united to God.

"The death of his sister was the signal of departure for himself. He survived her only forty days. A violent fever having seized him, he caused himself to be carried into the chapel of S. John the Baptist. He had before ordered to be opened the tomb in which his sister slept. There, supported in the arms of his disciples, he received the viaticum: then, placing himself at the side of the open grave, at the foot of the altar, and with his arms extended towards heaven, he died standing, murmuring a last prayer.

"Died standing!—such a victorious death became well the great soldier of God."[3]

He was buried beside his sister, on the very spot where had stood the altar of Apollo which he had cast down.

[3] Montalembert: Monks of the West, Book iv. c. 1.

IX

S. BRIDGET

One would have to look through many centuries, and over a wide tract of the earth's surface, to find a woman who possessed in her own generation so large an influence, and who so deeply impressed her personality on after generations, as S. Bridget. A woman she was, with no advantages of birth; but who by the mere force of character and her marvellous holiness, became a predominating power in the Church of Ireland after the death of S. Patrick.

It is said of the sick that the nurse is as important as the doctor; and in the spread of the Gospel and the establishment of the Church, the part of Bridget was only second to that of the great Apostle of Ireland.

The lives of S. Bridget that we possess are, unhappily, late, and intermixed, nay, overloaded with fable; the most grotesque and preposterous miracles are attributed to her. Nevertheless, when sifted, and the extravagances have been eliminated, sufficient of truth, of real history and biography remains behind for us to distinguish the main outline of her story, and to discern the real characteristics of the Saint.

It would seem to be a law of Divine providence, that at such periods of transformation as arise periodically, suitable persons should rise to prominence for giving direction to the disturbed minds of men in the general dislocation of received ideas.

To understand the exact position of S. Bridget, and the work she wrought, it is necessary for us to look at the condition of Ireland before it received the Gospel.

The whole political organisation was tribal, and not territorial. The chief of the clan was almost absolute, and about him, as a centre of unity, the tribesmen clung, as bees about their queen.

The chiefs had their Druids or Medicine-men, who blessed their undertakings and cursed their enemies, and the most unbounded confidence was placed in the efficacy of these blessings or curses. The Druids were endowed with lands, and probably in Ireland, as in Britain, constituted sacred tribes within the tribal confines of the secular chiefs.

When S. Patrick arrived he at once strove to effect the conversion of the chiefs, for without that his efforts with the bulk of the population must fail, and the conversion of a chief entailed as a consequence that of his clan. The Druids, when discredited, were disposed to accept Christianity; where they were not, the chiefs did not disestablish them, but gave to S. Patrick and his followers fresh sites on which to constitute their own ecclesiastical federations, on precisely the same system as that of the Druids. S. Patrick throughout acted in the most conciliatory spirit; he overthrew nothing that was capable of being adapted, and his wise forbearance conciliated even those at first most opposed to him.

There can be little doubt that in Ireland, as in Gaul, there had been colleges of Druidesses, as there had been of Druids. We do not know this by the testimony of texts, but it is more than probable. In Gaul these women were prophetesses; they lived in solitary places, often on islands. The nine Scenæ occupied an island in the Seine. The priestesses of the Namnetes lived on another at the mouth of the Loire, in huts about a temple. Once in the year they were bound, between one night and another, to destroy and replace the roof of their temple; and woe to the woman who dropped any of the sacred materials! Instantly she was set upon by her sisters, and torn limb from limb.

When S. Patrick and his missionaries entered on the prerogatives of the Druids, there was occasion for Christian women to usurp the places, and to some extent the functions, of the Druidesses. And this is precisely the line adopted by S. Bridget. The year of her birth was between 451 and 458, and she was the daughter of a slave woman, who had been sold to a Druid. Her mother's name was Brotseach. The father, Dubtach, was a nominal Christian, but a thoroughly heartless and unprincipled man.

The Druid and his wife were kindly people, and provided a white cow with red ears, on whose milk the little child was reared, and they allowed only one woman whom they could trust to milk the cow. As she grew up, Bridget was set to keep sheep on the moors; and there, not only did she tend them, but she also tamed the wild birds that flew about her. Soon the wild ducks and brent-geese allowed her to stroke them. When she had grown old enough to be useful, she asked leave to go and see her father, who lived in Leinster, whereas her mother was a slave in Ulster. The Druid at once gave her leave, and she left. Her father was not cordial in his reception of her, and set her to keep swine, and also at times to manage the kitchen. On one occasion, when visited by an acquaintance, he bade her boil five pieces of bacon for the entertainment. Unfortunately a hungry dog came in and carried off some of the bacon. This threw Dubtach into a fury, and he sent her back to her mother.

On her return, Bridget found Brotseach very ill and unable to attend to her work. It was summer, and she had been sent with the cattle to a mountain pasture, such as in Wales is called a hafod, whereas the winter habitation is the hendrê. There were twelve cows to be milked, and their butter to be made. Bridget undertook the supervision of the dairy with energy, and some verses have been preserved which it is said she sang as she churned: "Oh, my Prince, who canst do all things, and God, bless, I pray Thee, my kitchen with Thy right hand—my kitchen, the kitchen blessed by the white God, blessed by the Mighty King, a kitchen stocked with butter. Son of Mercy, my Friend, come and look upon my kitchen, and give me abundance."

It was reported to the Druid that Bridget gave the buttermilk to the poor, and he and his wife started for the mountain dairy to see that she was not wasting their substance; but they found that the butter she had made was so good and so plentiful that they were satisfied. Indeed, the kindly old man at once gave Brotseach and Bridget their liberty, to go where they would. He and his wife had been won by their piety and blameless life, and gladly consented to be baptised.

Bridget and her mother left with thanks and tears, and went to Leinster to Dubtach, who was well connected and rich, but avaricious. Bridget particularly annoyed him by her readiness to give food to the poor. To what extent she was justified in this may be questioned. But it must be remembered that the period was one in which no provision whatever was made for the poor, who starved unless assisted; and the girl's tender heart could not endure to see their sufferings and not to relieve them.

At last Dubtach could stand it no longer, and he took her in his chariot to sell her into slavery, to grind at the quern for Dunlaing, son of the King of Leinster. On reaching the king's dun, or castle, Dubtach went within and left Bridget outside in the chariot. A squalid leper came up, begging. Bridget, whether out of impulsive charity, or more probably in a fit of mischievous cunning, knowing that her father was selling her like a calf or a sheep, gave to the leper the sword which Dubtach had left in the chariot. The poor man at once disappeared with the gift. Next moment the prince and her father issued from the dun; the prince desired to look at the girl before purchasing her. Instantly Dubtach discovered that his sword was gone, and he asked after it. "I have given it away for your soul's good," said Bridget, with a twinkle in her eye. "On my word!" exclaimed the prince, "I cannot afford to buy such extravagant slaves as this."

Dubtach drove home in a fury, and he made his house so intolerable that she resolved to embrace the monastic life. She sought Bishop Maccaille, taking seven companions with her, all desiring to unite in the service of God and in ministering to the sick and needy.

Bishop Maccaille placed white veils on their heads, and blessed and consecrated them. Bridget was then aged eighteen.

Each of the girls chose one of the Beatitudes as her special virtue, which before all others she would seek to attain; and Bridget selected as hers "Blessed are the merciful, for they shall obtain mercy."

An odd story was told in later times concerning this consecration. It was said that Maccaille opened his book in the wrong place, and instead of reading the office for the consecration of a virgin, read over her that for the ordination of a bishop.

This fable was invented for a purpose. As we shall see presently, Bridget became head of an ecclesiastical tribe, and had under her jurisdiction a bishop who was amenable to her orders. This was a condition of affairs not at all uncommon among the British, Irish, and Scots, but it was incomprehensible in mediæval times to those trained under another system, when bishops were sources of jurisdiction. So this story was made up to give some justification for the exercise, by the Abbess Bridget, of authority over a bishop and priests.

In the Life of S. Bridget we are assured that when she was twelve years old she met S. Patrick, and that she wove the shroud in which he was buried. According to the ordinary computation, S. Patrick came to Ireland in 432, and died in 465; but Dr. Todd has shown good reason to believe that this calculation rests on an error. Palladius, whose name was also Patricius, was sent to Ireland in 432 by Pope Celestine; but he failed in his mission, abandoned Ireland, and died at Fordun. Neither S. Patrick himself, in his Confession, nor the earliest notices of him, say a word of his having been sent by Celestine, and there is reason to believe that he really came to Ireland in 460, and died in 493. If this be the case, it is quite possible that there may be truth in the story of the meeting of Bridget and the great apostle, and that it was his influence which induced her to adopt the life she chose. Bridget was now at the head of her little community of eight virgins, and they at once devoted themselves to good works.

Very soon great numbers of pious women came to her from every quarter, entreating to be received into her community and placed under her direction.

We can see by the brutality of Dubtach selling the mother of his child to a heathen Druid, though he himself professed to be a Christian, and later, deliberately attempting to sell his daughter, that women at that time were treated as chattels, and no respect was paid to them. It was largely due to Bridget that an immense revulsion of feeling in this particular took place.

She travelled over Ireland, and, wherever she was able, planted those who placed themselves in her hands near their own relatives and in their own country. She entered into correspondence with the bishops. She was warmly seconded by Erc of Slane, by Mel of Armagh, and Ailbe of Emly.

She managed to dot her settlements through a large portion of the island, and they became not only hospitals for the sick, but nurseries of learning, for she made a point of having the young girls confided to her for education taught their letters.

King Conall visited her on his way to make a raid, and to ask her benediction on his arms; "for," said he, "it is a mighty great pleasure cutting the throats of our enemies."

Bridget used all her endeavours to dissuade him from an unprovoked attack against those who were at peace with him, but she could induce him to go home only on one condition—that she would promise him her aid in all legitimate wars.

Somewhat later he was engaged in a military expedition, and it had been successful.

As he was returning, very tired, with his men, he reached a dun or castle, and resolved to rest there. His men dissuaded him, as the enemy were in pursuit. "Bah!" said Conall, "Bridget has promised to look after me," and he threw himself down to sleep. A great fire was lighted, and his men ranged the heads of the slain they had brought with them round the fire, and they themselves sat up talking and singing. Meanwhile the enemy came on, but they sent a spy, who crept unobserved up to the walls and looked in. When he saw the dead faces with the flicker of the red fire on them, and that Conall's men were alert, his heart failed him, and he went back and told his fellows that they must not risk a night attack on the dun.

Many touching stories are told of Bridget's tenderness to the sick: of a poor consumptive boy whom she nursed; of a man who carried his mother on his back for many days, that he might lay her before Bridget in the hopes that she might be healed of the lung complaint that afflicted her.

One day—so says the legend—two lepers came to her, and she bade the one wash the other. And he who was washed became whole. Then said she, "Go and wash thy brother." "Not I, forsooth!" replied the man. "I, a clean man, with sound skin, shall I scrub that loathsome object?" "Then I will do it," said Bridget; and she took the poor leper and thoroughly cleansed him.

The truth of this story would seem to be that Bridget bade a servant wash the leper, that he refused, and she herself performed the office.

But she did more than attend to the sick. She saved the lives of men condemned to death. On one occasion, a cupbearer to the King of Teffia let fall a valuable goblet, and it was dented. The king, in a rage, ordered the man to execution, though Bishop Mel interceded for him, but in vain; then Bridget got the cup, and, as she had skilful smiths under her, had the dents removed, so that it presented the same appearance as before, and the king was then reluctantly induced to pardon the man.

She was for a long time under the direction of Erc of Slane, in Munster. Whilst there, a certain anchorite, who had made a vow never to look on the face of a woman, started with his disciples to go to one of the Western Isles, there to establish a community. His way led near where Bridget was. Night fell, and his disciples, not relishing spending the hours of darkness on the open waste, and supperless, begged him to ask Bridget to give them food and lodging for the night. The old man absolutely refused. Bridget heard of this, and when the whole company was asleep she and one or two of her maids went on tiptoe to them and carried off all their bundles of goods and garments. When the men woke next morning everything was gone. Here was a pretty kettle of fish! Most reluctantly the old anchorite was obliged to swallow his objections and go humbly to Bridget and beg for the restitution of the packages. "Very well," said she, "when I have fed and housed you for a couple of days, you shall have them,—and do not hold up your nose and despise women any more." So she entertained the whole party, and when they departed she provided them with a couple of sumpter horses to carry their bundles for them. When the anchorite arrived at the island to which he had taken a fancy, to his dismay he found that a man lived on it with his wife and sons and daughters, and claimed it as his property, and absolutely refused to leave. The anchorite was forced to send for Bridget to arrange terms, and she with difficulty bought off the proprietor. "After all," said she, "you can't do without the help of women—for all your foolish vow."

When with S. Erc, she must have been in that portion of King's County that then belonged to the kingdom of Meath. After that she removed to Waterford, and remained for some time at Kilbride, near Tramore.

She heard that the King of Munster had a captive in chains very harshly treated. She went to his castle to beg for the man's release, but the king was not at home. However, the foster-father and -mother, and foster-brothers were there. They could give her no assistance. "I will await the king's return," said Bridget. Time began to pass heavily. She looked round, and saw that harps hung in the hall. "Come," said she, "let us have some music." The foster-parents of the king expressed themselves unwilling and incapable. But Bridget would take no excuse. Towards evening the king returned, and as he neared his hall, heard the twang of harps and voices singing and laughing. He came in at the door, and when he saw his foster-father with a cracked voice piping out an old ballad he laughed till the tears ran down his cheeks. Every one was in good humour, and he could not refuse Bridget her request.

Bridget next moved into Leinster, apparently to the district of Kinsale. She had not seen her father for some time, so now she went to visit him. He was not more amiable as he advanced in years. With difficulty she withdrew from him a servant maid, whom he was thrashing unmercifully. When she left, the maid said to her, "Oh! would to heaven you were always here, to save us from the master's violence!"

She—who had been a slave-girl herself—was pitiful to these poor things. Some runaway slave-girls took refuge with her, and she had hard work sometimes to reconcile their mistresses to leaving them under her protection.

Before she left her father, the old fellow asked her to get the king to let him keep as his own property a sword the prince had lent him. Bridget went to the castle. No sooner had she arrived than one of the king's men entreated her to take him into her tribe. So she asked the king to give her the man, and give her father the sword.

"You ask a great deal," said he. "I must have something in return."

"Shall I demand of God for you Life Eternal, and a continuation of royalty in your house?"

"As to Life Eternal," said the king, "I know nothing about it; and as to royalty after I am dead, the boys of my family must fight for their own crowns. Give me victory over my enemies."

"I will obtain that for you," she said. And on this being promised he acceded to both her requests.

This is a very characteristic story of an Irish saint. The kings and princes firmly believed that the saints could give them a place in heaven and victory over their foes, could continue their line in power, or deprive their posterity of sovereign rights.

This king was Illand, son of Dunlaing. Soon after this interview he went into the plain of Breagh, west of Dublin, where he fought the Ulster men and defeated them. After this he waged as many as thirty battles in Ireland, and gained eight victories in Britain. He died in 506. On his death the clan of Niall, taking courage, gathered their forces to attack the men of Leinster, who actually dug up the body of the old king, set it in a chariot, clothed in his regal garments, and marched against the men of the north, headed by the corpse.

Bridget now went into Connaught, and founded an establishment there. It was whilst there that an incident characteristic of the times occurred.

She had under her charge a poor decrepit woman who was failing rapidly. "The old creature can't live," said one of Bridget's women. "Let us strip her at once. It is bitter weather and frosty, and it will be awkward to get her garments off her back when she is stiff and stark."

"On no account," said Bridget. And when the cripple died she with her own hands divested the body of its clothing, then laid the garments outside the door in the frost, and washed them finally herself.

Bridget and some of her spiritual daughters paid a visit to S. Ibar of Begery. He served them at supper with bacon. Bridget saw two of the girls sitting with their platters before them and their noses turned up; they would not touch the food. She was very angry, jumped up from her seat, caught them by the shoulders, and turned them out of the hall, and bade them stand there, one on each side of the door, till supper was over. She had run short of seed-corn, and had gone to beg some of Ibar. The season was probably Lent, and the scruple of the girls was on that account.

When S. Bridget first saw the great plain of Breagh stretched before her, it was in early summer, and it was as though snowed over with the white clover, and the air that breathed from it was sweet with scent and musical with the hum of bees. She stood still, raised her hands in an ecstasy of delight, and said: "Oh! if this plain were but mine, I would give it all to God!"

"Good woman!" said S. Columba, when he was told this of Bridget. "God accepted the desire of her loving heart just as surely as if she really had made to Him the donation of all that land."

Once a bishop and a party of clerks arrived, and began to inquire when they were to have a meal and what they were to have to eat.

"It is all very well for you to be so clamorous," said Bridget, "for you are hungry. But can you not understand that I and my spiritual daughters are hungry also? We have no religious teacher here, and we long to hear the Word of God. Will you not give us who are hungry the nourishment of souls before you call on us to satisfy your stomachs?"

The bishop was ashamed, and led the way to the church.

It happened that there was a couple who led a cat-and-dog life, and at last declared that they could not live together, and that they would separate. Bridget went to them, and by her charm of manner and earnest words so won them over that thenceforth they came to love each other devotedly. So much so, that one day when the husband left home to cross an estuary, without saying good-bye, the wife ran after him into the water, and would have been drowned had he not returned to kiss her.

There was a madman who wandered on the mountain—Slive Forait. Bridget was crossing it, and her companions were in deadly fear of encountering the maniac. "I fear him not," said she; "I will go and find him."

Before long she encountered the poor wretch. She said to him, "My friend, have you anything to say to me?"

"Yes, nun," answered he: "Love the Lord, and all will love thee. Reverence the Lord, and all will reverence thee. I cannot avoid thee, O nun, thou art so pitiful to all the miserable and poor."

The life she led with the sisters was full of simplicity. She took her turn to tend the sheep, she helped to brew the Easter ale which she sent about to the bishops as her offering.

The following is a funny story.

Certain friends came to visit Bridget, and they left their house shut without a caretaker in it. When they were well away, some robbers came, broke open the byre and stole the oxen, and drove them away to the Liffey. They had to cross the river at a ford, but the water was deep, so the men stripped themselves, and that their garments might be kept dry, attached them to the horns of the cattle. But no sooner were the oxen in the water than they refused to proceed, and, turning, galloped home, carrying away the clothing of the robbers on their heads.

Having such large numbers of women under her direction, Bridget was obliged to draw up for them a set of rules. An odd legend attaches to the rules. She sent, so it was told, seven men and a poor blind boy, who was in her service, to Rome to obtain a rule. But as they were crossing the English Channel, the anchor caught. They drew lots who was to go down and release the anchor. The lot fell to the blind boy. He descended, unhooked the anchor, and it was hauled up, but left him behind. The seven went on, and returned at the end of the year, and were without any rule. As they were crossing the Channel, again the anchor caught, but it became disengaged, and up with it came the boy, and he had a Rule of Life with him, acquired in the depths, and this he took to Bridget, and it became her famous rule for all her communities. Perhaps the story originated thus. It was said that she had sent to Rome for a system of monastic discipline, but as none came to her, she fished up one out of the depths of her own conscience and common-sense.

Bridget certainly to the utmost strove to show forth the grace of Mercy, which she had elected as that for which she would specially strive, when she was veiled. Poor lepers were kept by her attached to her convent, and fed and administered to by her.

One day a woman brought her a hamper of apples. "Oh!" cried Bridget, "how pleased my lepers will be with them!" The woman angrily said, "I brought the apples for you, and not for a parcel of lepers."

On another occasion, when Bishop Conlaeth came to vest for the Eucharist, he found that his chasuble was gone. In fact, Bridget had cut it up and made of it a garment for a leper. Conlaeth was not overpleased. "I cannot celebrate without a proper vestment," said he. "Wait a moment," said Bridget, and ran away. Presently she returned with one she had made and embroidered with her own hands, and gave it to him in place of that she had disposed of to the leper.

A poor fellow who had gone to prefer a petition to the King of Leinster, saw a fox playing about in his cashel (i.e. castle). Not knowing that it was tame, and a pet of the king, he killed it. The king, Illand, was furious, threw the fellow into chains and vowed he would have him put to death. Bridget heard of it, and at once went to see him, and took with her a fox that had just been trapped. She offered the fox to Illand, on condition that he should let the man go. The king, supposing it was tame, consented. No sooner was the fellow released than Bridget let go her fox, when away dashed Reynard across the dun and over the walls, and was seen no more. "I have not got the best of this bargain," said the king.

In or about the year 480 she founded her mother house at Kildare—"The Cell of the Oak." She was granted land and a sanctuary, with jurisdiction over all who lived on her land. Thus she became a great ecclesiastical chieftainess, ruling not over women only, but over men as well. Indeed, it would seem that schools for youths were also under her. To regulate sacred matters in her tribe, she chose a bishop named Conlaeth, who was a good smith in the precious metals, and could manufacture bells.

In the great house of Kildare little children were taken charge of, either because orphans, or because given to the sisters by their parents. Tighernach, Bishop of Clones, was one of these. As a babe, Bridget held him at the font, and his infant years were under her care. He ever remained deeply attached to her. Perhaps it may be taken as a token of his affection that when he founded a church in

66

Cornwall, a chapel dedicated to his foster-mother should have been planted in proximity.

One who deeply reverenced her was the famous S. Brendan, who sailed for seven years on the Atlantic in quest of the Land of Promise. Once he was in conversation with her, and he said to her, "Tell me, Bridget, about your spiritual things. For my part I may say that, since I have learned to love and fear God, I have not stepped across nine furrows without my mind turning to Him."

Bridget thought for a moment and said, "I do not think, Brendan, that my mind has ever strayed from Him."

As her age advanced, her influence extended throughout Ireland. Swarms of her spiritual children must have crossed to Wales, to Devon and Cornwall, to Brittany, for we find in all these districts dedications to her; and these dedications signify churches placed under the rule of her congregation. It may indeed be said that it was she who initiated a great upheaval of woman from being a mere slave to become a revered member of the social body.

There was no woman in the British Church, either in Wales or Alba, which we now call Scotland, who occupied the same position. In Saxon England the only woman who at all approached her was S. Hilda, and she was not, like Bridget, an originator.

Conlaeth, Bridget's bishop, died in 519. She was sought, consulted by princes and by prelates. The sour Gildas, author of the "History of the Britons," if he did not pay her a visit, sent her as token of his esteem the present of a small bell, cast by himself.

Nothing particular is recorded of her last illness. She received the Communion from the hands of S. Nennid, whom years before she had gently reproved for his giddiness, and she died on February 1st, 525. According to some accounts she was aged seventy, according to others seventy-four.

There are two old Irish hymns in honour of her. One begins:
"Bridget, ever good woman,
Flame-golden, sparkling."
This is variously attributed to S. Columba, S. Ultan, and S. Brendan. The other hymn is by S. Broccan, who died in 650.

Both may be found in the Irish "Liber Hymnorum," recently issued by the "Henry Bradshaw Society."

X

THE DAUGHTERS OF BRIDGET

The story of the introduction of Christianity into Ireland is altogether so interesting, that it may be well to add something further to what has already been told of S. Bridget, and to the story of S. Itha. In the evangelisation of the Emerald Isle, woman had her place beside man, and S. Bridget and S. Itha played their part as effectually as did S. Patrick and S. Benignus.

Let us first see what the paganism of the Irish consisted in, and what was their social condition before S. Patrick preached, so that we may be able to realise to some degree what a revolution was effected by the introduction of the Gospel.

The heathen Irish certainly adored idols; one of the principal of these was Cromm Cruaich, which is said to have been the chief idol of Ireland. It is said to have been of gold, and to have been surrounded by twelve lesser idols of stone. To this Cromm Cruaich the Irish were wont to sacrifice their children. There still exists an old poem that mentions this:

> "Milk and corn
> They sought of him urgently,
> For a third of their offspring,
> Great was its horror and its wailing."

Then there were the Side worshipped. We do not know what these were, but it is thought that they were the spirits of ancestors. The sun also received adoration, so did wells. S. Patrick went to the well of Slan, and there he was told that the natives venerated it as a god; it was the King of Waters, and they believed that an old dead faith or prophet lay in it under a great stone that covered the well. S. Patrick moved the slab aside, and so destroyed the sanctity of the well.

There can be no doubt that polygamy existed: Bridget's father had a wife in addition to Brotseach, her mother; and S. Patrick, like S. Paul, had to insist that those whom he consecrated as bishops should be husbands of one wife.

Women were in low repute; they were required to go into battle and fight along with the men, and it was only on the urgency of Adamnan in the synod of Drumceatt, in 574, that they were exempted. A man could sell his daughter—it was so with Dubtach and Bridget. In the life of S. Illtyt, a Welsh Knight, it is told how one stormy morning, when he wanted to have his strayed horses collected, he pushed his wife out of her bed and sent her without any clothes on to drive the horses together. There is no doubt but the Irish husbands were quite as brutal.

There is a very curious story in the life of S. Patrick. He was desirous of revisiting his old master Miliuc with whom he had been a slave as a lad, and from whom he had run away. His hope was to convert Miliuc, and to propitiate him with a double ransom. But the old heathen, frightened at his approach, and unwilling to receive him and listen to his Gospel, burned himself alive in his house with all his substance. This seems to point to the Indian Dharna having been customary in Ireland.

When S. Patrick converted the Irish he dealt very gently with such of their customs as were harmless. The wells they so reverenced he converted into baptisteries, and the pillar-stones they venerated he rendered less objectionable by cutting crosses on them. The Druids wore white raiment, and had their heads tonsured; he made his clergy adopt both the white habit and the tonsure.

The oak was an object of reverence, and S. Bridget set up her cell under an ancient oak. She did not cut it down, and when people came on pilgrimage to it, taught them of Christ, from under its leafy boughs.

There was another relic of paganism that was not ruthlessly rejected. The ancient Irish venerated fire. Now, in Ireland, where the atmosphere is so charged with moisture, it is not easy to procure fire by rubbing sticks together, as it would be in Italy or Africa. Consequently it was a matter of extreme importance that fires should not be allowed to be extinguished. It was the custom among the early Latins that there should be in every village a circular hut in which the fire was kept ever burning, and the unmarried girls were expected and obliged to attend to it; and if by the fault of any it became extinguished, then her life was forfeit.

As the Romans became more civilised, the central hut was called the Temple of Vesta, or Hestia,—the Hearth-fire; and a certain number of virgins was chosen, and invested with great privileges, whose duty it was never to allow it to die out.

Now, it was much the same in Ireland, and it was more important there to keep fire always burning, than it was in the drier air of Italy. S. Bridget undertook that she and her nuns should keep the sacred fire from extinction, and Kildare became the centre from which fire could always be procured. The fire was twice extinguished, once by the Normans and again at the Reformation, finally.

The monastery of Kildare had a les about it—that is to say, it was enclosed within a bank and moat; the buildings were, however, of wood and wattle. This we know from a story in the Life of S. Bridget. When she was about laying out her monastery, a hundred horses arrived laden with "peeled rods," for Ailill, son of that very prince Dunlaing who had refused to buy her when he found she had given away her father's sword. Some of the girls ran to beg for the poles, but were refused. As, however, some of the horses fell down under their burdens, which were excessive, Ailill gave way and supplied them with stakes and wattles. He very good-naturedly allowed his horses to bring to Bridget as many more as were required, free of cost. "And," says the writer, "therewith was built S. Bridget's great house in Kildare."

All the sisters wore white flannel habits, and on their heads white veils. Each had her own cell, but all met for Divine worship and for meals. During the latter, Bridget's bishop Conlaeth read aloud to them.

Bridget travelled about a great deal, visiting her several communities, in a car or chariot; and her driver was at her desire ordained priest, so that as she sat in her conveyance, he could turn his head over his shoulder and preach to her and the sisters with her. One day Bridget said: "This is inconvenient. Turn bodily about, that we may hear you the better, and as for the reins, throw them down. The horses will jog along."

So he cast the reins over the front of the chariot, and addressed his discourse to them with his back to the horses. Unhappily, one of these latter took advantage of the occasion, and slipped its neck from the yoke, and ran free; and so engrossed were Bridget and her companion in the sermon of the priestly coachman, that they discovered nothing till they were nearly upset.

On another occasion, she and one of her nuns were being driven over a common near the Liffey, when they came to a long hedge, for a man had enclosed a portion of the common. But Bridget's driver had no relish for such encroachments, and determined to assert his "right of way," so he prepared to drive over the hedge. Bridget told him to go round, but not he—he would assert his right. Over went the chariot with such a bounce, that away flew the coachman, Bridget, and her nun, like rockets; and when they picked themselves up were all badly bruised, and Bridget's head was cut open. She had it bound up, and continued her journey. When she got home she consulted her physician, who with shrewd sense said, "Leave it alone. Nature is your best doctor."

In the "Book of Leinster," compiled in the twelfth century, is a list of saintly virgins who were trained under S. Bridget. It is, however, by no means complete. A few words shall be devoted to some of them. One, very young, had been committed to Bridget when quite a child. Her name was Darlugdach. She slept with Bridget, her foster-mother. Now, as she grew to be a big girl, she became restive, and impatient of the restraints of the convent life at Kildare, and she had formed a plan with another to run away.

The night on which she had resolved on leaving the monastery she was, as usual, sleeping in the same bed with Bridget; and she laid herself in her bosom, her heart fluttering with excitement, and with her mind at conflict between love of her foster-mother and desire to be out and free as a bird.

At last she rose, and in an agony of uncertainty cast herself on her knees, and besought God to strengthen her to remain where she knew she would be safe. Then, in the vehemence of her resolve, she thrust her naked feet before the red coals that glowed on the hearth, and held them there till she could bear it no longer, and limped back to bed, and nestled again into the bosom of the holy mother.

When morning broke, Bridget rose, and looked at the scorched soles of Darlugdach, and touching them said gently, "I was not asleep, my darling child. I was awake and aware of your struggle, but I allowed you to fight it out bravely by yourself. Now that you have conquered, you need not fear this temptation again."

Darlugdach, when S. Bridget was dying, clung to her, in floods of tears, and entreated her spiritual mother to allow her to die with her. But S. Bridget promised that she should follow speedily—but not yet. Now, on the very anniversary of S. Bridget's departure, next year, Darlugdach fell ill of a fever and died.

Another of Bridget's nuns was named Dara, who was blind—indeed, had been born without sight.

One evening Bridget and Dara sat together and talked all night of the joys of Paradise. And their hearts were so full that the hours of darkness passed without their being aware how time sped; and lo! above the Wicklow mountains rose the golden sun, and in the glorious light the sky flashed, and the river glittered, and all creation awoke. Then Bridget sighed, because she knew that Dara's eyes were closed to all this beauty. So—the legend tells—she bowed her head in prayer; and presently God wrought a great miracle, for the eyes of the blind woman opened, and she saw the golden ball in the east, and the purple mountains, the trees, and the flowers glittering in the morning dew. She cried out with delight. Now for the first time she—

"Saw a bush of flowering elder,
And dog-daisies in its shade,
Tufted meadow-sweet entangled
In a blushing wild-rose braid.

"Saw a distant sheet of water
Flashing like a fallen sun;
Saw the winking of the ripples
Where the mountain torrents run.

"Saw the peaceful arch of heaven,
With a cloudlet on the blue,
Like a white bird winging homeward
With its feathers drenched in dew."

Then Dara tried to lift up her heart to God in thanksgiving;
but her attention was distracted,—now it was a bird, then a flower,
then a change in the light,—and she could not fix her mind on God.
Then a sadness came upon her, and she cried—

"'O my Saviour!'
With a sudden grief oppressed,—
'Be Thy will, not mine, accomplished;
Give me what Thou deemest best.'

"Then once more the clouds descended,
And the eyes again waxed dark;
All the splendour of the sunlight
Faded to a dying spark.

"But the closèd heart expanded
Like the flower that blooms at night
Whilst, as Philomel, the spirit
Chanted to the waning light."

Again, another of Bridget's nuns was Brunseach; she,
however, went, probably on Bridget's death, to a religious house
that had been founded by S. Kieran of Saighir, over which he had set
his mother, Liadhain.

She was young and beautiful, and Dioma, the chief of the
country of the Hy Fiachach, came by violence and carried her off to
his dun or castle.

Kieran was angry, and at once seizing his staff, went to the
residence of the prince, and demanded that she should be

surrendered to him. The chief shut his gates and refused to admit the saint. Kieran remained outside, although it was winter, and declared he would not return without her.

During the night there was a heavy fall of snow, but the saint would not leave. Then Dioma, taunting him, said, "Come, I will let her go on one condition, that to-morrow I hear the stork, and that he awake me from sleep."

And actually next morning there was a stork perched on the palisade of the dun, and was uttering its peculiar cries. The tyrant arose in alarm, threw himself before the saint, and dismissed the damsel.

However, he had quailed only for a while, and presently renewed his persecution. Brunseach, according to the legend, died of fright, but was brought to life again by S. Kieran—that is to say, she fainted and was revived.

The story is late, and has become invested in fable; but so much of it is true, that Brunseach was carried off by Dioma, and that Kieran managed to get her restored.

It was perhaps through the annoyance caused by the prince that he resolved to leave Ireland. He settled in Cornwall. But he had taken with him his old nurse and Brunseach, and he found for them suitable habitations there. Kieran himself was there called Piran, and he founded several churches. That of his nurse in the Cornish peninsula is Ladock, and Brunseach is known there as S. Buriana.

"Nothing has been recorded of her life and labours in Cornwall, except the general tradition that she spent her days in good works and great sanctity; but the place where she dwelt was regarded as holy ground for centuries, and can still be pointed out. It lies about a mile south-east of the parish church which bears her name, beside a rivulet on the farm of Bosleven; and the spot is called the Sentry, or Sanctuary. The crumbling ruins of an ancient structure still remain there, and traces of extensive foundations have been found adjoining them. If not the actual ruins, they probably occupy the site of the oratory in which Athelstan, after vanquishing the Cornish king, knelt at the shrine of the saint, and made his memorable vow that, if God would crown his expedition to the Scilly Isles with success, he would on his return build and endow there a church and college in token of his gratitude, and in memory of his victories.

"It was on that wild headland, about four miles from Land's End, that S. Buriana took up her abode; and a group of saints from Ireland, who were probably her friends and companions, and who seem to have landed on our shores at the same time, occupied contiguous parts of the same district. There she watched and prayed with such devotion, that the fame of her goodness found its way back to her native land; and thenceforth Brunseach the Slender, by which designation she had been known there, was enrolled in the catalogue of the Irish saints; but her Christian zeal was spent in the Cornish parish that perpetuates her name."[4]

Bridget had two disciples of the name of Brig or Briga. This was by no means an uncommon name. A sister of S. Brendan was so called.

Another was Kiara, and this virgin we perhaps meet with again in Cornwall as Piala, the sister of Fingar. Amongst the Welsh and Cornish the hard sound K became P, thus Ken (head), was pronounced Pen; so S. Kieran became Piran.

Fingar and his sister formed a part of a great colony of emigrants who started for Cornwall. Fingar had settled in Brittany, but he returned to Ireland and persuaded his sister to leave the country with him. This she was the more inclined to do as she was being forced into marriage in spite of her monastic vows. They left Ireland with the intention of going back to Brittany, but were carried by adverse winds to Cornwall, and landed at Hayle.

King Tewdrig, who had a palace hard by, did not relish the arrival of a host of Irish, and he set upon them and massacred most of them. Kiara, however, was not molested, though her brother was killed. She settled where is now the parish church of Phillack. The scene of her brother's martyrdom was Gwynear, hard by. She probably did not care to leave the proximity to his grave; she had no one to go with to Armorica, and it seems likely that a larger body of Irish came over shortly after, occupied all the west part of Cornwall, and so made her condition more tolerable.

---

4 Adams, "Chronicles of Cornish Saints," in the Journal of the Royal Institution of Cornwall, 1873.

XI

S. ITHA

What Bridget was for Leinster, that was Itha or Ita for Munster; and from the way in which her cult spread through Devon and Cornwall, we are led to suspect that there were a good many religious houses and churches in the ancient kingdom of Damnonia that were under her rule, and looked to Killeedy in Limerick as their mother-house.

S. Itha was a shoot of the royal family of the Nandesi, in the present county of Waterford. Her father's name was Kennfoelad, and her mother's was Nect. They were Christians, as appears from the fact of S. Itha having been baptised in childhood.

She was born about 480, and probably at an early date received the veil "in the Church of God of the clan."

Unfortunately we have not the life of S. Itha in a very early form; it comes to us sadly corrupted with late fables foisted in to magnify the miraculous powers of the saint.

She moved to the foot of Mount Luachra, in Hy Conaill, and founded the monastery of Cluain Credhuil, now Killeedy, in a wild and solitary region, backed by the mountains of Mullaghareirk, and on a stream that is a confluent of the Deel, which falls into the Shannon at Askaton.

The chief of the clan or sept of Hy Conaill offered her a considerable tract of land for the support of her establishment, but she refused to receive more than was sufficient for a modest garden.

Let us try to get some idea of what one of these monasteries was like.

In the first place a ditch and a bank were drawn round the space that was to be occupied, and the summit of the bank was further protected by a palisade of stakes with osier wattling. In such places as were stony, and where no earthwork could well be made, in place of a bank, there was a wall.

Within the enclosure were a number of beehive-shaped cells, either of wattle or of stone and turf. Certainly the favourite style of building was with wood; but of course all such wooden structures have perished, whereas some of those of stone have been preserved. There were churches, apparently small, and a refectory, bakehouses, and a brewery and storehouses.

Outside the defensive wall of enclosure lived the retainers of the abbey. Where an abbot or abbess was head of an ecclesiastical tribe, he or she was bound to find land for each household: nine furrows of arable land, nine of bog, nine of grass-land, and as much of forest. As the population increased, a secular or an ecclesiastical chief was obliged to obtain an extension of territory, or would be held to have forfeited his claims as a chief. This led to incessant feud among the Celtic princes; it forced the saints to be continually striving to obtain fresh grants of land and make fresh settlements. When there was no more chance of obtaining land in Ireland, they sent swarms to Britain and to Brittany, to found colonies there, under the jurisdiction of the saint. This explains the way in which the Celtic saints were incessantly moving about. They were forced to do so to extend their lands so as to find farms for their vassals.

A very terrible story is told of the condition of affairs in Ireland in 657. The population of the island had increased to such an extent that the chiefs could not find land enough for the people. Dermot and Blaithmac, the kings, summoned an assembly of clergy and nobles to discuss the situation and consider a remedy. They concluded that the "elders" should put up prayer to the Almighty to send a pestilence, "to reduce the number of the lower class, that the rest might live in comfort." S. Fechin of Fore, on being consulted, approved of this extraordinary petition. And the prayer was answered from heaven, but the vengeance of God fell mainly on the nobles and clergy, for the Yellow Plague which ensued, which swept away at least a third of the population, fell with special heaviness on the nobles and clergy, of whom multitudes, including the two kings and S. Fechin of Fore, were carried off.

S. Itha does not seem to have coveted land, and she assumed a different position from that taken by S. Bridget. She was not an independent chieftainess over a sacred tribe, but acted as prophetess to the secular tribe of the Hy Conaill. Just as among the Germans, the warriors had their wise women who attended the tribe, blessed the arms of the warriors, and uttered oracles, so was it among the Celts; and we are assured that the entire sept, or clan, unanimously adopted S. Itha as their religious directress and, in fact, wise woman. In such cases, when a prophecy came true, when a military undertaking blessed by the Saint proved successful, the usage was, that an award was made in perpetuity to him or to her, a tax imposed that must be paid regularly by the tribe.

Thus there were two ways by which a Celtic saint might subsist—either as an independent chieftain over a sacred tribe, or as the patroness or prophetess of a tribe, not owning much land, but drawing a revenue from the sept or clan.

We have a very curious illustration of this in the life of S. Findcua, who was the great seer and prophet of Munster. He blessed the arms of the king seven times in as many battles, and was rewarded for each; he received tribute in this wise: "The first calf, and the first lamb, and the first pig," from every farm for ever. "For every homestead a sack of malt, with a corresponding supply of food yearly."

Now there is not a trace of S. Itha having allowed herself on any occasion to degrade herself to blessing and cursing, blessing the arms of the Leinster men and covering their foes with imprecations. She succeeded in inspiring the whole of the people with such reverence, that they were ready to receive what she declared as a message from God, and she used this position for no other object than that of advancing God's kingdom, stirring up to good works, encouraging peace, and restraining violence. She showed no eagerness for gifts. On one occasion a wealthy man, to whom she had rendered a service, insisted on forcing money on her. She at once withdrew her hand, absolutely refused it, and to show him her determination, washed her hands that, she said, had been defiled by contact with his filthy lucre. God's gifts were not to be traded with, and profit must not be made out of an office such as that filled by her.

Parents, desirous of having their children brought up to the ecclesiastical state, committed them to her; and thus she became the foster-mother of S. Pulcherius or Mochoemoc, of S. Cumine, and S. Brendan. The latter was committed to her when one year old, and she kept him with her till he was five. Throughout his life Brendan retained not merely the tenderest love for Itha, but such a reverence that he consulted her in all matters of importance.

One day Brendan asked her what three works were, in her opinion, most well-pleasing to God. She replied, "Faith out of a pure heart, sincerity of life, and tender charity."

"And what," further asked Brendan, "what are most displeasing to God?"

"A spiteful tongue, a love of what smacks of evil, and avarice," was her ready reply.

Brendan, as a little fellow, was the pet of the community, and all the sisters loved to have him and dance him in their arms. In the life of S. Brendan is inserted a snatch from an older Irish ballad concerning him:

> "Angels in shape of virgins white
> This little babe did tend.
> From hand to hand, fair forms of light,
> Sweet faces o'er him bend."

S. Erc, Bishop of Slane, seems to have been Itha's principal adviser and friend; and when the five years of Brendan's fostering were over, Erc took the little boy away to teach him the Psalms and the Gospels. S. Erc found it rather hard to keep the boy supplied with milk, but a hind with her fawn, so says the legend, was caught, and gave her milk to Brendan.

It may be asked, What was the mode of life of the community of S. Itha?

Unhappily we do not know so much of that of the religious women as we do of that of the monasteries of men, yet we cannot doubt that the rule of the house for women much resembled that in the others. Here is an account of the order as given in the life of S. Brioc, an Irishman by race, though born in Cardigan.

"At fixed hours they all assembled in the church to celebrate divine worship. After the office of vespers (6 p.m.) they refreshed their bodies by a common meal. Then, having said compline, they dispersed in silence to their beds. At midnight they rose and assembled to sing devoutly psalms and hymns to the glory of God. Then they returned to their beds. But at cockcrow, at the sound of the bell, they sprang from their couches to sing lauds. From the conclusion of this office to the second hour (8 a.m.) they were engaged in spiritual exercises and prayer. Then they cheerfully betook them to manual labour."

Happily one of the monastic offices of the early Irish Church has been deciphered from a nearly obliterated leaf of the Irish MS. Book of Mulling: it consisted of the Magnificat. What preceded this is illegible: some verses of a hymn; the reading of the Beatitudes from the Sermon on the Mount, a hymn of S. Secundinus, a commemoration of S. Patrick, a portion of a hymn by S. Hilary of Poitiers, the Apostles' Creed, the Lord's prayer, and a collect.

The work of the day consisted in teaching the young girls their letters, in needlework, tending the cattle—in which each, abbess included, took turn—grinding corn in the handmill, and cultivating the garden.

Numerous visitors arrived to consult S. Itha, and she most certainly had fixed hours in which to receive them.

One striking instance of the veneration in which she was held is that S. Coemgen of Glendalough, when dying, sent to entreat her to come to him; he would have no one else minister to him in his last sickness, and he begged her, when he expired to place her hand over his mouth and close it.

One Beoan was a famous artificer; he was a native of Connaught. He went to Itha and passed into her service; but was summoned by his military chief to attend him in one of his raids. He

78

departed most reluctantly. Itha was greatly distressed at losing him. As he did not return after a skirmish, she went to the scene of the encounter, and found him grievously wounded, but still living. Under her fostering care he recovered. According to late legend, his head had been cut off and thrown away. She found his body but not his head, so she called "Beoan! Beoan!" Whereupon the head came flying through the air to her, and she set it on again. So a very simple transaction was magnified into a ridiculous fable.

After leaving her, S. Brendan went about with Bishop Erc in his waggon, from which the bishop preached to the people. One day when Erc was addressing a crowd, Brendan was in the back of the waggon, looking over the side, clearly not attending to the sermon. Then a small, fair-haired, rosy-faced girl came near, and seeing the little fellow peeping over the side, she tried to scramble up the waggon-wheel to get to Brendan and play with him. But he laid hold of the reins and lashed her with them, so that she was forced to desist, and fell back crying. Erc was much annoyed at Brendan's conduct, and sent him into the black-hole in punishment.

Some years later, Itha required Brendan to come to her: she was in great trouble, and needed his assistance. He went accordingly, and with many tears she told him that one of her pupils had run away some time before, and had fallen into very bad courses, which had led at last to her being reduced to be a slave-girl in Connaught. Would he go in search of her and bring her back, with assurance that everything would be forgiven and forgotten?

Brendan readily undertook the task, and succeeded in redeeming the girl and restoring her to her spiritual mother.

Now Brendan himself got into trouble. He had gone with a boat one day to an island, taking with him two lads, one quite young. He left one boy in charge of the boat, and advanced up the land with the other. Then this latter said to him, "Master, the tide will rise before we get back, and I am sure my little brother cannot manage the boat alone."

"Be silent," retorted Brendan. "Do you suppose that I do not care for him as much as you do yourself?"

After a while the young man returned to the matter. "I am sure," said he, "it is not safe to leave the boy unassisted. The current runs very strong."

"Bad luck to you!" said Brendan, flaming up,—he was a peppery man,—"Go yourself, then;" and the youth took him at his word and found the boy struggling with the boat, tide and wind were driving from shore, and he was unable to control the coracle. The elder ran into the water to assist his brother, and a great wave

79

swept him off his feet and he was drowned, but the little boy escaped.

After this S. Brendan had no peace of mind. He thought himself responsible for the loss of the youth. He had wished him "Bad luck," and bad luck indeed had fallen to him.

He went at once to his foster-mother, and consulted her.

It is quite possible that the relatives of the drowned youth had taken the matter up, and pursued Brendan in blood-feud. So Itha, after mature consideration, advised Brendan to leave Ireland for a while; and in punishment for his hastiness, and for having caused the death of the youth, she bade him abstain from blood in everything.

So Brendan started. He went to Armorica, and determined to visit Gildas, the historian, who was then at his abbey of Rhuys. Gildas was a sour, ill-tempered man, very hard; and when Brendan arrived, it was just after sundown and the gates of the monastery were closed. He announced who he was—a traveller from Ireland—but Gildas replied that rules must be kept, and it was against his rule to open after set of sun, so Brendan was constrained to spend the night outside the gates.

Thence he went to Dol, but after a while, and a visit to S. David in Wales, he returned to Ireland, and now Itha told him a marvellous story. There was a rumour that far away to the west beyond the horizon was a wondrous land of beauty. He must not remain in Ireland: let him put to sea, sail after the sun as it set, and discover the mysterious land beyond the Atlantic.

The imagination of Brendan was fired; he set to work to construct three large vessels of wickerwork, and he covered them with skins; each vessel contained thirty men—some were clergy, a good many laymen—and he took a fool with him, because he begged hard to be admitted. Brendan was absent three or five years, it is uncertain which—for apparently the time of his absence in Brittany is included in one of the computations.

Wonderful stories are told of what he saw and did, but no trust can be put in the narrative. On his return he went to Itha to report himself. She received him with great pleasure, but objected that he had not literally obeyed her, for his sails had been made of the skins of beasts, so had been the covering of his boats, and cattle had been slaughtered for the purpose, so that he had not wholly abstained from blood.

But it is doubtful whether this is what she really said. It is probably the legend writer's explanation for what follows. "Why," asked Itha, "should you risk these lengthy voyages in such frail vessels as coracles made of basket-work covered with hides? Next time build boats of wood."

This was a new idea. The Irish, like the Welsh, had hitherto used large coracles, and the only wooden boats they had employed were trunks of trees hollowed out, and these only on lakes.

Brendan at once seized on the suggestion, and constructed ships of wood, which were the first ever built in Ireland, and these were due to the idea of S. Itha.

Brendan made a second voyage to the land beyond the ocean, and it is possible that he may have actually reached America; but, as already said, nothing trustworthy has come to us of the result of his attempts.

Itha had a brother, S. Finan, and she was related to S. Senan of Achadh-coel.

Itha in her old age was attacked by perhaps the most terrible and painful disease to which poor suffering mortality is subject, and it is one to which women fall victims more often than men. She was attacked in her breast, but endured her pains night and day with the utmost patience and trust in God's mercy. Her nuns were affected to tears at her sufferings, but she had always a smile and cheerful words on her lips to banish their discouragement.

She died at length on January 15th, in the year 569 or 570, and was laid in her church of Cluain Credhuil, which has since borne the name of Killeedy or the Church of Ida.

She must have been known beyond the island of Ireland, for in the Salisbury Martyrology she is entered in strange form as "In Ireland the festival of S. Dorothea, also called Sith (S. Ith)" on January 15th.

In Cornwall a lofty and bare hill, that commands the Atlantic and the coast, is crowned by a great ruined camp. It had belonged to the British, but was wrested from them and became a stronghold of the Saxons, who held it so as to dominate the entire neighbourhood. This is Hellborough, not far from Camelford. It continued to be a royal castle, the property of the Crown, though it does not seem that any mediæval castle was built upon it. Now, curiously enough, in the midst of this great camp is a mound of stone or cairn, and on this cairn is a little chapel, at present in ruins, dedicated to the saint whose life has just been given. And on the river Camel, that flows into the Padstow estuary, is a parish that bears the name, though corrupted into S. Issey. But near Exeter is a parish church that has her as patroness with the name unmutilated, as S. Ide.

How came these dedications in Cornwall and Devon? Either because S. Brendan on his way home from Brittany founded the churches in memory of his dear foster-mother, or else because here were colonies of holy women from the mother-house in Limerick.

In or about 656 Cuimin of Connor wrote the "Characteristics of the Irish Saints" in metre, and this is what he says of Itha:—

> "My (dear) Itha, much beloved of fosterage,
> Firmly rooted in humility, but never base,
> Laid not her cheek to the ground,
> Ever, ever full of the love of God."

XII

S. HILDA

Hilda was born in 614. She was the daughter of Hereric, nephew of Edwin, king of Northumbria.

Her childhood was darkened by the civil wars that rent Northumbria, at this time divided into two kingdoms, each engaged in fighting the other for supremacy.

In 627, when aged thirteen, she received baptism, along with her uncle Edwin, at the hands of S. Paulinus. She lived thirty-three years in her family, "very nobly," says Bede, and then resolved to dedicate the rest of her life to God. Her intention was to go to Chelles, in France, for her training; and, for this purpose, she went into East Anglia to its queen, her sister.

She spent a year in preparation for her final exile; but her purpose was frustrated by a summons from S. Aidan, the Apostle of Northumbria, to return to her own country and settle there. She obeyed at once, and was placed by Aidan as superior over a few sisters in a small monastic settlement on the north bank of the Wear. But she was there for a year only, when she was called to replace S. Heiu, the first Abbess of Hartlepool. This was in 649.

At Hartlepool, the Saint's care was to introduce order and discipline, which had, apparently, been relaxed under Heiu. Hither came her mother, who passed the rest of her days under the rule and care of her daughter, and there she died and was buried.

In some excavations carried on at Hartlepool on the site of the old abbey, between 1833 and 1843, among a number of Anglo-Saxon tombs that were discovered, some bore the names of Berchtgitha, Hildigitha, and other members of the sisterhood.[5]

So great was Hilda's reputation for spiritual wisdom, that when King Oswy, in fulfilment of his vow, consecrated his daughter, Elfleda, to Almighty God, as a thank-offering for his victory over Penda, King of the Mercians, it was to S. Hilda's care that he committed her.

Whether now or later is uncertain, but she had a second convent at Hackness, where some very remarkable relics of the ecclesiastical foundations of Hilda still remain.

In 658, the peace and security of Northumbria had been

---

[5] Notes on the History of S. Bega and S. Hild. (Hartlepool, 1844.) By D. H. Haigh.

secured by the final victory gained by Oswy over the Mercians, at Winwaed. Hilda at once took advantage of the king's vow to give a certain number of farms to God, to secure Streaneshalch, now Whitby, for the establishment of a new and larger monastery.

M. de Montalembert, the historian of Western Monachism, says that: "Of all sites chosen by monastic architects, after that of Monte Cassino, I know none grander and more picturesque than that of Whitby. Nothing now remains of the Saxon monastery, but more than half the Abbey-church, restored by the Percies in the time of the Normans, still stands, and enables the marvelling spectator to form for himself an idea of the solemn grandeur of the great edifice.... The beautiful colour of the stone, half-eaten away by the sea-winds, adds to the charm of these ruins. A more picturesque effect could not be imagined than that of the distant horizon of azure sea, viewed through the gaunt, hollow eyes of the ruinous arches."

Here, for thirty years, the great Hilda ruled. She must have been a woman of commanding character, and of no mean mental power, for she exercised a really marvellous influence over bishops, kings and nobles. They came to consult her, and received her advice with respect. "All who knew her," says Bede, "called her Mother, on account of her singular piety and grace. She was not merely an example of good life to those who lived in her monastery, but she afforded occasion of amendment and salvation to many who lived at a distance, to whom was carried the fame of her industry and virtue."

The story went that before her birth her mother had dreamt that she had in her lap a jewel that sent forth streams of light; and it was proudly thought that this meant that she would nurse Hilda, precious as a gem, and diffusing the light of divine truth through dark Northumbria.

Under Hilda's charge at Whitby was the little Elfleda, daughter of Oswy, who was to succeed her in the abbacy.

The monastery was a curious institution. It was double. There was a community of women and another of men. There was, however, but one church in which they met for prayer. If we may judge by the Celtic monasteries elsewhere, a wall separated the monks from the nuns, so that they could hear but not see each other.

The monastery for men under Hilda became a nursery for bishops. Thence issued Bosa, who became Bishop of York,—Hedda, Bishop of Dorchester, but afterwards translated to Winchester; Oftfor, Bishop of Worcester, and John of Hexham,—all saints; also Wilfrid II., afterwards of York.

How these double monasteries were managed one would have been glad to learn, but very few details concerning them remain.

At Whitby, where she had to govern both men and women, her powers of organisation and control were conspicuous. But she had others under her beside monks and nuns: she ruled a large number of serfs with their families, attached to the soil and tilling it.

Amongst these was an old cowherd, named Caedmon. He was, as a serf, very ignorant and uneducated, but he had rare natural gifts, long unsuspected. He attended the carouses so dear to the beer-drinking Saxons and Angles, but he was unable to take his part, whenever the harp was handed to him and it was his turn to sing a ballad. On such occasions, mortified, he had been wont to rise from his place, and retire to his own reed-thatched cottage, where he slept beside the cows in their stall.

But one evening, when he had done this, as he was lying among the straw, and the oxen were beside him chewing the cud, and the air was sweet with their breath, he fancied, half-asleep and half-awake, that he heard a voice say: "Sing me something."

Then he replied: "How can I sing? I have left the feast because I am so ignorant that I cannot."

"Sing, nevertheless," he thought the vision said.

"But—what can I sing about?"

"Sing the story of the World's Birth."

Then, somehow, an inspiration came on him, and in the night, among the cows, out of the straw, he raised his voice, and began to throw into rude verse the story of Creation. It was very rugged, but very fresh, and it welled up from his heart; in the morning he thought over the lines he had composed, and during the day talked of his newly-acquired powers.

The Abbess Hilda heard of it, and she sent for him, and he recited his poem before her.

Whether at the time he twanged the harp we do not know; probably he drew his fingers across the strings as he finished each line, so as to give time for him to form or remember the next.

Now, in this poetry there was no rhyme, as we understand it. The musical effect was produced by alliteration—that is to say, by the repetition of some ringing consonant or broad diphthong, usually at the beginning of a word. If we understood Anglo-Saxon music, we should understand the charm to the ear of this alliteration.

Hilda at once recognised the genius of the old cow-herd; she took him into her household, and bade him devote himself to the cultivation of his talent. Thus it is due to her that Anglo-Saxon poetry took its rise—or, at all events, was recognised as literature deserving of being preserved. Caedmon's poems are the earliest specimens we have.

But Hilda, with real genius, saw at once in the faculty of the old peasant a great means of conveying to the rude people the story of Scripture and the lessons of the Gospel. They were quite incapable of reading. Priests were few, and widely scattered. The people loved ballads; they would hearken for hours, sitting over the fire, to a singer who twanged the strings and then sang a stave or a line. They loved a long story. It could not be too long for them, having no books, nothing wherewith to relieve the tedium of the long winter evenings.

Now, thought Hilda, if we can run the Bible stories into ballad form, these will be sung in every cottage and farm wherever a gleeman can go certain of welcome; they will be eagerly listened to. So she gave to Caedmon clergy who translated the Scripture narrative from Latin into homespun Saxon. He listened, took his harp, the fire came into his grey eyes, and he sang it all in verse. Ninety-nine out of a hundred other women would have said, "This is very interesting, but the man must be snubbed; he is only a keeper of cows, and he must be taught not to presume." Hilda, however, was above such pettiness: seeing a divine gift of song, though granted to quite a common poor man, she at once endeavoured to ripen it, and to turn it to a practical, good end. How to seize an occasion, an opportunity, and make use of it, is not given to all.

Another instance of Hilda's clear mind and sound sense was in the settlement of the vexed question of Easter.

About that I shall have more to say when we come to the story of S. Elfleda.

The British-Irish Church did not observe Easter on the same day as the Roman Church; and as the Mercians and Northumbrians had received their Christianity from Iona, the metropolis of the Scottish Church, they kept the festival at one time, when the men of Kent and Wessex kept it at another. This produced discord at the very season when minds should be awed and calm; and it was a constant source of bickering and religious quarrels. The situation was intolerable, and, probably at the instigation of Hilda, a parliament was convoked at Whitby in 664 to settle the difficulty. This was the Witenagemot, composed of the principal nobles and ecclesiastics of the country, and presided over by the king.

Hilda was now fifty years old, and one would have supposed at that age would have adhered with the utmost tenacity to the rule in which she had been brought up, and which had been observed by her Father-in-God, S. Aidan, and by S. Cuthbert, whom she revered as a saint and a prophet inspired by the Divine Spirit. But she was a woman too sensible and too forbearing to force her own likings on the Church, against what her judgment told her was right. Pope Honorius had written in 634 to the Irish, exhorting them "not to think their small number, lodged at the utmost fringe of the world, wiser than all the ancient and modern Churches throughout the earth." Even in Iona great searchings of heart had begun. S. Cummian had written to the abbot there, explaining how the error arose whereby the two Churches were separated, and he entreated the Celtic clergy to give way. "What," he asked, "can be worse thought concerning the Church, our mother, than that we should say, Rome errs, Jerusalem errs, Alexandria errs, Antioch errs, the whole world errs; the Scots and Britons alone know what is right."

Hilda's leanings were entirely to the Scottish side, but Oswy strongly adopted the other, and the nobles and freemen, not caring much one way or the other, held up their hands to express their willingness to observe Easter at such time as pleased the king.

Hilda seems at once to have submitted, and to have introduced the observance of the Roman computation at Whitby, but the northern bishops withdrew, unconvinced and discouraged. Hilda was almost certainly alive when Caedmon died, but she was not long in following him. For the last seven years of her life she suffered greatly; then, says Bede, "the distemper turning inwards, she approached her last day, and about cock-crow, having received the Holy Communion, to further her on her journey, and having called together the servants of Christ that were in the same monastery, she admonished them to preserve evangelical peace among themselves and with all others; and as she was speaking she saw Death approaching, and—passed from death to life." She died in 680.

XIII

S. ELFLEDA

When the terrible Penda had advanced into Northumbria, against Oswy, destroying homesteads and harvests with fire, and butchering all who fell into his hands, then the Northumbrian king sent presents to him, and asked for peace. The fierce Mercian refused the presents offered: nothing would satisfy him but the absolute subjection of the Northern Kingdom. Then, in despair, Oswy vowed to God that, as the old Pagan had rejected his gifts, he would dedicate his little one-year-old daughter to Him, together with twelve farms, if He would bless his arms in battle.

The odds were against Oswy. The host opposed to him was thrice as numerous as his own. Ethelhere, King of the East Angles, had come to the aid of Penda; and Odilwald, son of S. Oswald, who had been given an underlordship of part of Deira, and who thought he ought to have succeeded his father in kingship, went over to Penda.

The battle was fought on the Winwaed, near Leeds; the Mercians and their allies in their confidence had incautiously put the river at their back. Heavy rains filled it to overflow; it became a deep and boiling torrent, cutting off retreat. The Mercians were defeated. A panic fell on them, and as they fled they were swept away by the swollen river. Of the thirty eorldormen who marched with Penda, hardly one survived. The King of the East Angles and the savage old Mercian were among those who were slain. Odilwald did not enter the battle. He was well aware that when Bernicia had been eaten, Penda's next mouthful would be Deira. He bore a bitter grudge against Oswy, but for all that did not care to put the knife into the hand of the Mercian king wherewith to have his own throat cut.

A battle song was composed on the occasion, of which a snatch has been preserved:—

"In the river Winwaed is avenged the slaughter of Anna,
The slaughter of Sigbert and Ecgric as well,
The slaughter of Oswald and Edwin who fell."

The battle was fought in 655, consequently S. Elfleda was born in 654.

Oswy faithfully kept his vow. He set apart twelve estates to be thenceforth monastic property—six in the north and six in the south of his double kingdom. He then surrendered the little Elfleda to be brought up to the service of God.

Her mother was Eanfleda, daughter of Edwin, the first Christian King of Northumbria. It was, in fact, her birth, on Easter Day, 626, which was the occasion of the subsequent conversion of her father, and of his subjects; and Eanfleda was the firstfruits of her nation to receive baptism on the Whit Sunday following.

Oswy, the father of Elfleda, was a dissolute and murderous ruffian, who in cold blood had murdered the gallant Oswin, King of Deira, the kinsman of his own wife.

Oswy gave his daughter to S. Hilda, at Hartlepool.

In the furious and fratricidal wars which were waged in England by the conquerors of the British, each kingdom was animated by a blind instinct that the unity of the race should be effected somehow; but each understood this only as by bringing the rest under subjection.

Elfleda is described by Bede as a very pious princess. She had a sister, older than herself, Alcfleda, who had been married to Peada, son of the ravager Penda. But Alcfleda bore no love to her husband, and had him assassinated whilst he was celebrating Easter.

Two years after Elfleda had been placed at Hartlepool, S. Hilda obtained a grant of land where now stands Whitby, but which was then called Streaneshalch. She moved thither, and there constituted her famous monastery. This was in 658.

With Hilda remained Elfleda till the death of the great abbess in 680. On the death of Oswy in 670, ten years before, her mother Eanfleda came there; but when Hilda died, the young Elfleda, and not her mother, was elected to be the second abbess. As she was scarcely twenty-five, she was guided and assisted by Trumwin, who had been Bishop of Witherne, but had been obliged to leave his diocese by the unruly Picts, and he had withdrawn to the monastery of Hilda to remain under her rule.

Like all the Anglo-Saxon princesses of the period who retired into the cloister, Elfleda did not cease to take a passionate interest in the affairs of her race and her country, and to exercise a very remarkable influence over the princes and the people. When in 670 Oswy died he was succeeded by his son Egfrid, as unprincipled a man as his father. In 674, at Easter, S. Cuthbert was drawn from his island and cell and was ordained Bishop, with his seat at Lindisfarne, to rule the Northumbrian Church, in the presence of the king, at York. It was then that Cuthbert, knowing what was in the heart of the turbulent king, urged him to refrain from attacking the Picts and Scots, who were not molesting the Northumbrians. He would not, however, hearken. He had already despatched an army under Beorf to wantonly ravage Ireland. This had, as Bede said, "miserably wasted that harmless nation, which had always been friendly to the English; insomuch that in their hostile rage they spared neither churches nor monasteries." The expedition against the Picts was determined on against the advice of all his friends, and of the Bishop of York, and of Cuthbert.

Elfleda was in great anxiety about her headstrong brother, and she went to see Cuthbert concerning him. He and the abbess met, having gone by sea to the place appointed for the interview. She threw herself at his feet and entreated him to tell her what the issue would be—would Egfrid have a long reign?

"I am surprised," answered Cuthbert, "that a woman well versed, like you, in the Scriptures, should speak to me of length of human life, which lasts no longer than a spider's web. How short, then, must life be for a man who has but a year to live, and has death at his door!"

At these words Elfleda's tears began to flow. She felt that the wise old hermit saw that the mad as well as wicked expedition of her brother must end fatally.

Presently, drying her tears, she continued with feminine boldness to inquire who would be the king's successor, since he had neither sons nor brothers.

"Say not so," replied Cuthbert. "He shall have a successor whom you will love, as you as a sister love Egfrid."

"Tell me," pursued Elfleda, "where can this successor be?"

Then he turned his eyes to the islands dotting this coast, and said: "How many islands there be in this mighty ocean! Surely thence can God bring a man to reign over the English."

Elfleda then perceived that he spoke of a young man, Alcfrid, supposed to be the son of her father Oswy by an Irish mother, and who had been a friend of Wilfrid, and was now in Iona, probably hiding from his brother, whom he could not trust.

The venerable Cuthbert was not out in his conjecture. On May 20th, 684, Egfrid was drawn into a pass at Drumnechtan, in Forfar, was surrounded by the Scots and Picts, slain, and the great bulk of his men cut to pieces.

"From that time," says Bede, "the hopes of the English crown began to waver and retrograde; for the Picts recovered their own lands, which had been held by the English."

Alcfrid at once left Iona, and was chosen king. He was a good and just prince, much under the influence of Wilfrid and inclined to adopt Roman fashions.

It becomes necessary now to speak of a controversy that rent the unity of the Church in England.

All Northumbria, Mercia and Essex had received the faith from Iona, the monastic capital of the Scots, whereas Kent and Wessex had received it from Rome.

Iona had been founded in 563 by S. Columba, an Irishman; and it was from Iona that S. Aidan, the Apostle of Northumbria, had been sent. Lindisfarne, the seat of the Bishops of Northumbria, was a daughter of Iona.

Now, there were certain differences between this Celtic Church and that of Rome and Gaul.

In the first place, the Britons and Irish had been cut off from communication with the rest of Europe by the troubles that afflicted the Empire as it fell into ruin under the blows of the Barbarians. Consequently they were unaware that a change had been agreed on in the observance of Easter. It was discovered in 387 that the system of calculating Easter was erroneous, and Pope Hilary employed one Victorinus to frame a new cycle, which was thenceforth followed in the Latin Church. But of this change the British and Irish Church knew nothing; and when Augustine and his followers arrived in Kent they found that the ancient Church of the Britons observed Easter on a different day from themselves.

That was not all. The Celtic monks had a different tonsure or mode of cutting of the hair from the Latin monks. Instead of shaving the top of the head, and leaving the hair as a crown, they shaved the front of the head from ear to ear. Now, the reason of the use of the tonsure among the Celts was this. The cutting of the hair signified adoption, and there is some reason to believe that every tribe or clan clipped its hair in its own peculiar fashion. The Ecclesiastical tribe adopted the shaving of the front of the head; and every one so shaven belonged in the ecclesiastical clan.

When S. David settled in the valley where is now the Cathedral that bears his name, there was an Irish Pict invader living in a camp hard by. He had seized on that bit of Pembrokeshire. His name was Boia, and he was a pagan. His wife was highly incensed at Christian monks settling on their land and near at hand, and she tried to goad her husband to murder them. But he was a good-natured man, and he absolutely refused to do her will. Then she resolved to get her heathen gods to strike them dead, and in order to gain the favour of the gods she must offer them a sacrifice of one of her children. But she had none of her own; so she called to her a little girl, a daughter of her husband by a former wife, and told her she would cut her hair. She took the girl down into a sunny place in a hazel grove on the slope of the hill, and there, with her shears, cut

91

her hair. Now, as cutting the hair was esteemed to be adoption, by this act she had made the child her own; so she instantly with the shears cut the girl's throat as an offering to the gods. Now the British clergy, by their form of cutting the hair, regarded themselves as adopted into the family of God, or the Ecclesiastical tribe.

Augustine and the Latin clergy could not understand this. Instead of arguing with the native Christians they denounced them. They called them Judaisers because they observed Easter at the wrong time, which was false; and they called the tonsure of the Celts that of Simon Magus, which was nonsense.

There were other peculiarities. The British Church used unleavened bread at the Eucharist, and the Latin Church at that time only such bread as was leavened. Also, another high misdemeanour was that, instead of employing a single collect before the Epistle and Gospel, there were more than one said. In these two last particulars the Latin Church has altered now her practice; in the matter of the unleavened bread, the change took place in the tenth century.

Now, the matter of Easter was very vexing, for whilst those who followed the Roman rule were singing Allelujah and were rejoicing, the Celtic and Northumbrian and Mercian Christians were still keeping Lent. Precisely the same thing occurs in Russia, where in English and Roman chaplaincies Easter is kept whilst the Russians are still fasting.

This became a burning question when the Northumbrian kings married princesses from the South. These had their own chaplains and kept Easter at their time, whilst their husbands and the court and the people were in the midst of Passion solemnities.

As to the matter of the tonsure, on which the Roman clergy made a great noise, it was like asking a clan to change its tartan,—say the McDonalds to be forced to adopt that of the Campbells.

Oswy had found the condition of affairs intolerable, as his own queen followed the Roman rule, whilst he observed that of the Celtic Church.

Oswy had associated his son Alcfrid with him in the government of Northumbria, and Alcfrid was much swayed by Wilfrid, a companion of his age then living at the Court of Oswy, who had been to Rome, seen its wonders and the splendours of the pontifical services in the old basilica of S. Peter. He came back with his head full of what he had seen, and utterly scorning everything British, even the Christianity of his Northumbrian brethren. In his idea nothing would avail but the conforming of the Church in Northumbria to Roman obedience and Roman customs.

Oswy was induced to summon a council at Whitby to decide

matters of controversy. On the Scottish side were S. Colman, the Northumbrian bishop, with his clergy; S. Hilda, followed of course by Elfleda; S. Cedd, bishop of the East Saxons. On the Roman side was Agilbert, bishop of the West Saxons, the Queen's chaplain, Wilfrid, then only a priest, one other priest, and a deacon. The King favoured the Celtic use, Alcfrid the Latin.

Wilfrid was the chief speaker on the latter side, and he dexterously appealed to Oswy's fears. The Roman Church must be right, he said, because S. Peter, its founder, held the keys of heaven. At once Oswy quaked; he recollected his dastardly murder of Oswin. It would never do for him not to make a friend of the doorkeeper of heaven. So he gave way, and the Celtic bishops, deprived of his support, but unyielding and unconvinced, withdrew.

It was now hoped that the Church would have peace, and the points of difference would gradually disappear. S. Hilda, at Whitby, accepted the Roman computation. But it was not so easy to satisfy a clergy and people brought up in another school.

To make matters worse, Wilfrid was appointed Bishop of York, a man of a violent, headstrong character, who, to begin with, refused to accept consecration from bishops in the North with Celtic orders; but went deliberately to Gaul to be ordained there, so as to cast a slur on the Church of the people to rule over whom he had been called.

Wilfrid had no idea of persuasion, had not a spark of Christian love in his composition; he could insult, browbeat, but not persuade. In his diocese he roused revolt and provoked brawls, and was expelled from it, not once only, but whenever he returned.

Now the new King Alcfrid had brought with him from Iona attachment to the order of the Church of SS. Columba and Aidan. Elfleda inherited the same reverence and love for these usages. But on the other side there were strong political reasons which led men to think it would be well to come to an arrangement with Canterbury and Rome. It was awkward to have these differences, this cleavage, even in the royal palace. It was unadvisable that the Angles of the North and of the Midlands should have to apply to the Scots and Britons, their hereditary enemies, for their bishops. If the Angles and Saxons could but agree in ecclesiastical matters, they would be a more compact body to oppose Britons and Scots; and, further still, it would be an element conducive to the much desired unity of the English people. This ecclesiastical unity would be the first step to the cessation of that internecine war between Northumbria, Mercia, and Wessex, which tore the island in pieces and soaked its fertile soil with blood.

Hoping that Wilfrid, now an aged man, would be softened by

adversity, he was suffered to return. To the new king, as well as to his sister, S. Elfleda, Abbess of Whitby, Archbishop Theodore of Canterbury wrote, to exhort them to receive Wilfrid with unreserved kindness. They consented, and in 687 he reappeared at York; but it was to excite new storms in his diocese, and he was again exiled in 691.

Alcfrid died in 705, and the Northumbrian crown passed to a prince named Eadwulf. Wilfrid had taken advantage of the death of Alcfrid to return, but was ordered to leave the country in six days. But Eadwulf was dethroned, and Osred, a son of Alcfrid, aged eight, became King of Bernicia. By some unexplained means Wilfrid was now, all at once, master of the situation. Archbishop Berthwald of Canterbury had convoked a synod that was to settle the disputes, and it met on the banks of the Nidd. It was attended by the northern Bishops of York, Lindisfarne, and Witherne, by Elfleda also, the Abbess of Whitby, and by Berchtfrid, the regent of the kingdom during the minority of Osred. Archbishop Berthwald read the letters of the pope on the points in dispute. But the bishops were very unwilling to make way for so turbulent a person as Wilfrid. Then it was that Elfleda stood forward, and in a voice which was listened to as an utterance from heaven, she described the last illness of her half-brother Alcfrid, and his death, and assured all that he had then resolved to accept the papal decrees, which hitherto, when his mind was clear, he had so vigorously rejected. "This," said she, "was the last will of Alcfrid the King. I attest the truth of it before Christ."

Nevertheless the three bishops would not yield; they retired from the assembly to confer among themselves, and with the Archbishop, and, above all, with the sagacious Elfleda. It was due to her that a compromise was effected. The monasteries of Ripon and Hexham were restored to Wilfrid and with that he was to be content.

Shortly before his death, S. Cuthbert went to see Elfleda in the neighbourhood of the great monastery of Whitby, to consecrate a church she had built there. They dined together; and during the meal, seeing the knife drop from the trembling hand of the old bishop, in the abstraction of his far-away thoughts, she asked him what he thought about, and he told her that he had had a glimpse of the future. She urged him to eat more.

"I cannot be eating all day long," he replied. "You must allow me a little rest."

On the death of Oswy, as already related, Elfleda's mother had come to Whitby and placed herself under the rule of her own daughter, and Elfleda closed her eyes. She herself died in 716, at the age of sixty-four. No account of her last illness has been transmitted to us.

Elfleda certainly played an important conciliatory part when minds were heated with controversy. She was right undoubtedly. It was a mistake for the Church in North England to hold to a usage that was founded on a blunder. It was a mistake to persist in keeping Wilfrid, canonically bishop of York, for many years out of his see. It was a political necessity that all Englishmen should be united, at all events, in their religious observances. That paved the way to future political unity.

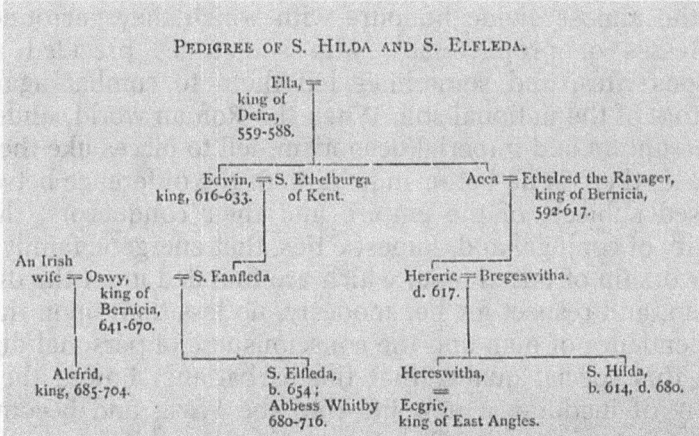

PEDIGREE OF S. HILDA AND S. ELFLEDA.

Ella, ⚭
king of
Deira,
559-588.

Edwin, ⚭ S. Ethelburga   Acca ⚭ Ethelred the Ravager,
king, 616-633.   of Kent.   king of Bernicia,
                                      592-617.

An Irish
wife ⚭ Oswy,   ⚭ S. Eanfleda   Hereric ⚭ Bregeswitha.
       king of   d. 617.
       Bernicia,
       641-670.

Alefrid,   S. Elfleda,   Hereswitha,   S. Hilda,
king, 685-704. b. 654;   ⚭   b. 614, d. 680.
                Abbess Whitby   Ecgric,
                680-716.   king of East Angles.

Pedigree of S. Hilda and S. Elfleda.

95

XIV

S. WERBURGA

The words of Montalembert deserve to be transcribed and re-read, so true are they as well as graceful.

"Nothing had more astonished the Romans than the austere chastity of the German women; the religious respect of the men for the partners of their labours and dangers, in peace as well as in war; and the almost divine honours with which they surrounded the priestesses or prophetesses, who sometimes presided at their religious rites, and sometimes led them to combat against the violators of the national soil. When the Roman world, undermined by corruption and imperial despotism, fell to pieces like the arch of a cloaca, there is no better indication of the difference between the debased subjects of the empire and their conquerors, than that sanctity of conjugal and domestic ties, that energetic family feeling, that worship of pure blood, which are founded upon the dignity of woman, and respect for her modesty, no less than upon the proud independence of man and the consciousness of personal dignity. It is by this special quality that the barbarians showed themselves worthy of instilling a new life into the West, and becoming the forerunners of the new Christian nations to which we all owe our birth.

"Who does not recall those Cimbri whom Marius had so much trouble in conquering, and whose women rivalled the men in boldness and heroism? Those women, who had followed their husbands to the war, gave the Romans a lesson in modesty and greatness of soul of which the future tools of the tyrants and the Cæsars were not worthy. They would surrender only on the promise of the consul that their honour should be protected, and that they should be given as slaves to the Vestals, thus putting themselves under the protection of those whom they regarded as virgins and priestesses. The great beginner of democratic dictatorship refused: upon which they killed themselves and their children, generously preferring death to shame.

"The Anglo-Saxons came from the same districts, bathed by the waters of the Northern Sea, which had been inhabited by the Cimbri, and showed themselves worthy of descent from them, as much by the irresistible onslaught of the warriors as by the indisputable power of their armies. No trace of the old Roman spirit which put a wife in manu, in the hand of her husband—that is to say, under his feet—is to be found among them. Woman is a person, and not a thing. She lives, she speaks, she acts for herself, guaranteed against the least outrage by severe penalties, and protected by universal respect. She inherits, she disposes of her possessions—sometimes even she deliberates, she fights, she governs, like the most proud and powerful of men. The influence of women has been nowhere more effectual, more fully recognised, or more enduring than among the Anglo-Saxons, and nowhere was it more legitimate or more happy."[6]

Britain had been invaded, and subdued. From the wall of Antonine that connected the Firth of Forth with the Clyde, to what was now to be called the English Channel, all the east coast and centre of the island was occupied by the conquerors from Germany. The Britons had been rolled back into the kingdoms of Strathclyde, Rheged, Wales, and Cornwall and Devon.

The conquerors had coalesced into three great kingdoms—Northumbria, Mercia, and Wessex.

From the island of Iona, missionaries of the Irish Church had effected the conversion of the Northumbrians. Augustine with his handful from Rome had introduced Christianity into the little subject Kingdom of Kent. From Northumbria the disciples of Iona penetrated Essex and made converts also there. But in Mercia Mid-England paganism was supreme, and the terrible Penda made himself paramount from the Thames and Wash to the Severn. The West Saxons were cowed.

But S. Oswald, the Northumbrian king, restored the older domination of Northumbria, only to fall again. For thirty years Penda flung himself with fury against the Northern kingdom, and devastated it with fire and sword. Towards the end of his long reign he entrusted the government of the Mid-Angles to his son Peada, who married Alcfleda, daughter of the Northumbrian king, and at the same time received baptism from the hands of the Celtic bishop Finan.

Thus Christianity began to infiltrate into Mid-England also from the North and from the Celtic Church; and missionaries from Lindisfarne followed him into his principality.

The savage old pagan Penda acquiesced—perhaps he thought it inevitable that England should become Christian. The Britons to a man believed. All Northumbria had submitted to the Cross; the conversion of the East Saxons and of Wessex was in full progress. Penda raised no opposition, but poured forth the vials of his scorn upon such as had been baptised, and who did not live up to their

---

[6] Monks of the West, 1868, vol. v., pp. 219-21.

baptismal promises. "Those who despise," said he, "the laws of the God in whom they believe, are despicable wretches."

But, notwithstanding the union by marriage between the families, the rivalry between Mercia and Northumbria could not be allayed; it must be decided on the battlefield. It was only when driven to desperation by the encroachments and insults of Penda, that Oswy resolved to engage in a final conflict with the man who had defeated and slain his two predecessors, Edwin and Oswald. During the thirteen years that had elapsed since the overthrow of Oswald, Penda had periodically subjected Northumbria to frightful devastations. Oswy, knowing his weakness, when the eighty-year-old pagan had got as far north as Bamborough, entreated for peace, and sent him a present of all the jewels and treasures of which he could dispose. Penda set them aside roughly, resolved, so it was believed, to root out and destroy the whole Northumbrian people. Then, in his despair, Oswy vowed—should God strengthen his hand and lead him to victory—that he would give his infant daughter to God and endow twelve monasteries. "Since the pagan will not take our gifts," he said, "let us offer them to One who will."

The battle of Winwaed resulted in the complete rout of the Mercians and their wholesale destruction, and Penda himself fell.

For the moment the ruin of Mercia seemed complete, and Oswy extended his supremacy over the whole of it. For three years the Mercians endured this foreign rule; but in 659 they surged up in revolt, drove the Northumbrian thanes from the land, and raised Wulfhere, a younger son of Penda, to the throne.

Under the able arm of this new king Mercia rose once more into a power even greater than that under Penda. Oswy died in 670, and thenceforth no Northumbrian king made any attempt to obtain the dominion over the Mid or Southern English.

During the three years after the death of Penda, Oswy had poured missionaries into Mercia. Peada had already brought the Irish monk Diuma with him, and he became bishop in Mercia. He was followed by another Irishman, Ceolach, a disciple of S. Columba. The third bishop was Trumhere, a Northumbrian abbot, consecrated at Lindisfarne. His successors, Jaruman and Ceadda, had also been ordained by the Scots.

In 658 Wulfhere had married Ermenilda, daughter of Ercombert, King of Kent, and of his wife S. Sexburga. This was just before the revolt which raised him to the throne. He does not seem to have been a Christian like his brother Peada, but to have felt much like old Penda, his father.

By her he had four children—Werburga, Ceonred, Rufinus, and Wulfhad.

Under a pious mother, Werburga grew up in the nurture and admonition of the Lord; and from an early age her great desire was to embrace the religious life, and spend her days in the peace of the cloister. It was a lawless and godless time. Men were coarse and cruel, the palace was a scene of drunkenness and riot, from which her gentle spirit shrank. She is described as being very lovely and sweet in manner. She daily assisted with her mother at Divine Service, and spent much of her time in reading and in prayer.

When she came of age to be married, her hand was sought by one Werebod, a thane about the court, but she refused him.

Now we come to a story about which some difficulties exist. In the twelfth century one Robert of Swaffham wrote an account of the death of Rufinus and Wulfhad, sons of Wulfhere and brothers of S. Werburga. The authority is late, too late to be trusted, as we do not know whence the writer drew his narrative.

According to this story, when Rufinus and Wulfhad heard of Werebod's proposal, they scouted it, and told him to his face that he was not worthy to have her. Werebod dissembled his mortification, and waited an opportunity for revenge. The princes were then at Stone, in Staffordshire, where Wulfhere had a palace.

One day Wulfhad was out hunting, when the stag he was pursuing brought him to the cell of S. Ceadda or Chad, who exhorted him to receive the faith of Christ and be baptised. Wulfhad answered that he would do so if the stag he had been pursuing would come of its own accord, with a rope round its neck, and present itself before him. S. Chad prayed, and the stag bounded through the bushes to the spot, with the rope as Wulfhad desired. S. Chad baptised the prince, and next morning communicated him. Rufinus was led by his brother to receive holy baptism, and when Werebod learned this, he told the king of it, and Wulfhere, in a fit of fury, pursued his sons to the cell of S. Chad, and killed them with his own hands.

The story as it stands is impossible. There is no early notice of it, so that it reposes on a late tradition. Nevertheless, that there is a basis of truth is most probable, if not certain. The Church of Kinver is dedicated to SS. Rufinus and Wulfhad, and it stands under the Kefnvaur, the great red sandstone ridge on which are earthworks where Wulfhere had one of his strongholds. This is probably the site of the murder. That the two princes in their youthful pride scouted the suit of Werebod and insulted him is likely enough. That they had received lively impressions of reverence for Christianity from their mother is also very probable. That they had placed themselves under instruction by S. Chad, and had been baptised by him, is also very likely. But that their father should have killed them on that

99

account is inadmissible. Werebod may have poisoned his mind against his sons, and represented them as plotting against him with the Northumbrian king and using Chad as an intermediary, and he may have goaded Wulfhere into ordering their death on that account; or there may have been a violent scene between them which ended in the king killing them; or, more likely still, Werebod may himself have waylaid and assassinated them whilst out hunting. It took very little among the Anglo-Saxons to transform any one who died a violent death into a martyr; and when two royal princes had been killed, some excuse for regarding them as witnesses to the faith was sought and invented.

The bodies of the princes were conveyed to Stone, so called because of a memorial set up over them by Wulfhere, an inscribed pillar-stone; but, moved by compunction, he founded there a religious house for women. Wulfhere himself was baptised, and gave his consent to his daughter retiring from the world. He also founded the great monastery of Medehamstead, afterwards Peterborough, as some expiation for his crime.

Before this, Wulfhere had been constantly engaged in extending the power of Mercia. He detached from Northumbria all the district south of the Mersey, and with it got hold of Chester, of which place in later times his daughter was to be regarded as patroness. He gained a hold on the whole of the Severn valley and the Wye, our Herefordshire, over which he set his brother Merewald as under-king. Then he fought the West Saxons under Cenwalch in 661, and defeated them in a signal battle, and extended his ravages into the heart of Wessex as far as Ashdown. Then he turned his arms east along the Thames valley, and brought the East Saxons and London under his sway. Still unsatisfied, he crossed the river into Surrey, subdued it, and invaded Sussex and forced the King Ethelwalch to submit, and to receive baptism. Werburga resolved to retire to Ely where her great-aunt Etheldreda was abbess. Wulfhere and his court conducted her thither, in great state.

We cannot now see Ely in anything like its ancient condition. Then the entire district from Cambridge to the Wash was one broken sheet of water dotted with islets. In places there were shallows where reeds grew dense, the islands were fringed with rushes and willows. The vast mere was a haunt of innumerable wild birds, and the water teemed with fishes. The vast plain of the fens— which is now in summer one sea of golden corn, in winter a black dreary fallow cut up like a chess-board into squares by dykes—was then a tangle of meres, rank growth of waterweeds and copses of alders and grey poplars. The rivers Cam and Nen lost themselves in the waste of waters. Trees torn up, fallen into the water, floated about, formed natural rafts, lodged, and diverted what little current there was in the streams.

Here and there poles had been driven into the stiff clay that formed the bottom of the swamp, cross-pieces had been tied to them, then platforms erected six, ten feet above the surface of the water, and on these platforms huts had been constructed of poles and rushes, in which lived families, their only means of communication with each other and with the firm land being by boat. On the water and by the water they lived, tilling little bits of land left dry in summer but submerged in winter.

The islets were outcrops of fertile land, natural parks, covered by the richest grass and stateliest trees, swarming with deer and roe, goat and boar, as the water around swarmed with otter and beaver, and with fowl of every feather and fish of every scale.

Of all these islets none could compare with Ely, not, as has been supposed, named from the eels that were found about it, but from the elves who were supposed to have chosen it for their own and to dance in the moonlight on its greensward.

Better, purer beings than elves, had taken possession of this enchanted isle—S. Etheldreda and her nuns; and it was through them that the wild fen-dwellers, those who lived on platforms above the water, received the rudiments of the faith, and were ministered to in their agues and rheumatic paralysis.

Etheldreda did not found her monastery here till 673. As Wulfhere died in 675, he can have accompanied his daughter there only very shortly after Etheldreda's settlement in the place. There is no stone anywhere near, every block that has been employed on the glorious cathedral has been brought from a distance, mostly from Barwell, in Northamptonshire.

Etheldreda constructed her monastery and church entirely of wood. Great trunks had been split and these split logs formed the sides of her church, and it was thatched with reeds from the marshes. The king came by boat; the oars flashed in the sun, and the water rippled as the vessels were driven through it to the landing stage. Werburga, eager, stood looking forward to the lovely island that seemed to float on the water; if, as is probable, she was born some time before Wulfhere became king, she would then be between twenty-eight and thirty. At the landing-stage was her great-aunt with her nuns, in black habits with white veils; and no sooner had Werburga descended from the boat than they struck up the Te Deum, and advanced, leading the way, singing, to their wooden church.

Now followed the usual trials: Werburga was first stripped of her costly apparel, her coronet was exchanged for a linen veil, purple and silks were replaced by a coarse woollen habit, and she resigned herself into the hands of her superior, her great-aunt, S. Etheldreda.

We know the form of the ceremonial, and the prayers used on such an occasion, but we do not know who the bishop was who consecrated Werburga.[7] She was led to the foot of the altar, after the reading of the Gospel, and was then asked for two public engagements which were indispensable to the validity of the act: in the first place, the consent of her parents, and in the next her own promise of obedience to himself and his successors. When this had been done he laid his hands upon her to bless her and consecrate her to God. After prayers he placed the veil on her head, saying, "Maiden, receive this veil, and mayest thou bear it stainless to the tribunal of Christ before whom bends every knee in heaven and on earth."

By the rules of the Anglo-Saxon Church the taking of the irrevocable vows was not suffered till the postulant had reached her twenty-sixth year, but we cannot be sure that this rule prevailed so early. The Celtic Church allowed it at the age of twelve.

When Wulfhere died, then Werburga's mother came also to Ely, and on the death of S. Etheldreda, in 679, her grandmother Sexburga, widow of Ercombert, king of Kent, became abbess, and ruled till 699, when she died, whereupon Werburga's mother succeeded. At one time three generations of princesses of the blood of Hengest and Odin were seen together in the peaceful isle of Ely, wearing the same monastic habit, and bowing in prayer in the same wooden church. Werburga lived long and happily as a simple nun under her grandmother's and mother's kindly rule and direction, till, on her mother's death, she was summoned to take the place of abbess.

It is very important for us to understand what was the moving principle at this period which led to the foundation of so many religious settlements. The Saxons and Angles had been a people living in war, loving war, and regarding the cutting of throats and the destruction by fire of every house and city as the highest vocation of a man. But when they had occupied the greatest portion of Britain, and further, when they had embraced Christianity, a change took place in their opinions. They came to see that there was some charm in peace, and dignity in the cultivation of the soil. But it was only after a struggle that they could stoop to take hold of the plough and lay aside the spear. They could be brought to this only

---

[7] Probably Seaxwulf, the Mercian bishop.

by example, and it was this which the monks and nuns issuing from their own princely, royal families showed them.

"In the monastic movement of this time," says Mr. Green, "two strangely contrasted impulses worked together to change the very aspect of the new England and the new English society. The one was the passion for solitude, the first outcome of the religious impulse given by the conversion; a passion for communing apart with themselves and with God which drove men into waste and woodland and desolate fen. The other was the equally new passion for social life on the part of the nation at large, the outcome of its settlement and well-doing on the conquered soil, and yet more of the influence of the new religion, coming as it did from the social civilisation of the older world, and insensibly drawing men together by the very form of its worship and its belief. The sanctity of the monastic settlements served in these early days of the new religion to ensure for them peace and safety in the midst of whatever war or social trouble might be disturbing the country about them; and the longing for a life of quiet industry, which we see telling from this moment upon the older English longing for war, drew men in crowds to these so-called monasteries."[8]

Wulfhere was succeeded in 675 by his brother Ethelred, a quiet, unambitious king, who devoted his energies to the foundation of monasteries, dotting them about Mercia with the object of softening and civilising a people that had the instincts of the beasts of prey. He entrusted his niece Werburga with a sort of general supremacy over all the nunneries in his kingdom. She visited them, regulated them, and brought them into order, before her mother's death and her own appointment to the abbacy of Ely. Thus she resided for a while at the head of the communities of Weedon, Trentham, and Hanbury.

One incident of her story may be quoted.

It happened that a shepherd at Weedon was being brutally maltreated by the steward. The daughter of a king flew to the spot, threw herself between the overseer and the poor wretch he was beating and kicking, and arrested his arm and thrust him back, and held him from his victim, till his passion subsided, and he retired shamefaced.

Werburga died at a ripe age at Trentham, on February 3rd, 699.

Two centuries later, in order to save her remains from the Danes, they were conveyed to Chester, where there was a collegiate church that had been founded by her father at her request. Her body was, however, laid in what is now the Cathedral.

---

[8] Green, The Making of England; ed. 1897, ii. p. 111.

XV

A PROPHETESS

Among the most remarkable people of the twelfth century, one who stood forth on the stage of history and exercised there a part of no little importance, Hildegarde, is not to be passed over. Yet, when one comes to study her, she is a person who strikes the student with perplexity. She was, indeed, a woman possible at all times, but only possible as one of significance in the century in which she lived.

She was one of those marvellous women who, indeed, occupied a somewhat analogous place among the ancient pagan Germans—a seeress, a prophetess, even a priestess, like Velleda or Ganna. She took up the same position in the Christian Middle Ages, directed, ruled, foretold, threatened, and was listened to in all seriousness. Popes, prelates, kings consulted her, and all quailed at her threats and denunciations. She saw visions and dreamed dreams; she endeavoured to throw rays of light to illumine the past as well as the future. She thought with her inspired eye to unveil the mysteries of creation. Uneducated, she dictated in Latin; uninstructed, she wrote on natural history; unordained, she preached sermons even to popes.

All kinds of people wrote to her on all kinds of subjects, and she solved their difficulties, advised them in their perplexities, illumined their ignorance.

She has had imitators in all after ages—Antoinette Bourgignon, Joanna Southcott, Krüdner, and Madame Blavatski—but none achieved such success, exercised so wide an influence, was treated with so much submission.

The Emperor, the princes, the nobility, the clergy, the people all believed in her prophetic power, and accepted her commands without a murmur. Her warnings and promises were received as divine revelations, although she spared no one in her denunciations.

The cause for this unbounded respect has been a matter of dispute, but is still inexplicable. That she was a coarse deceiver, who imposed herself on the people as inspired, by a long-continued course of deception, cannot for a moment be allowed by such as without prejudice examine her writings and her conduct. She was made a tool of, and a willing tool, by S. Bernard, to further the crusade he had at heart. But when, in spite of prophecy and promise, that crusade ended in hideous disaster and in dishonour as well, her influence with the people was not in the least shaken.

At the court of Count Meginhard of Spanheim lived the knight Hildebert of Böckelheim, his kinsman. Hildebert's wife Mathilda bore him in 1098 a daughter, who was named Hildegarde, on their estate a little above Kreuznach on the Rhine. She was the tenth child, and her parents were no little concerned how to provide for such a fry. The simple expedient in those days was to send some of the family into monasteries and convents. From an early date Hildegarde was destined to be a nun. She, together with her kinswoman Chiltrude, the daughter of the count, were sent to be reared by Jutta, the abbess of S. Disibod, a sister of Count Meginhard. Jutta was an uneducated woman; learning was of no account in her convent, and Hildegarde was brought up in ignorance of nearly everything that a young woman of good family ought to have acquired even in the twelfth century.

That Hildegarde was hysterical cannot be doubted, but hysteria is precisely the most mysterious of all ailments. The phenomena connected with it are the perplexity of physicians even at this day. Many and ponderous works have been written upon it in England, France especially, and Germany, but it remains still an unsolved puzzle.

From a very early age she saw visions, and when she spoke of them to her playfellows, and they stared at her and did not appear to comprehend what she said, she shrank into herself and refrained from communicating to others the things that she saw and heard, or fancied she saw and heard. Even at the age of five, this singular gift was noticed by her parents, who could not understand it. Jutta made the girl learn the Psalms in Latin, and she obtained some glimmer of an idea what the words meant, but she did not even acquire a knowledge of the alphabet, nor that of reading music.

Hildegarde was constantly unwell, but her aches and pains were apparently due to hysteria and nothing else, and the suppressed desire to be doing something, making her personality felt, which was impossible as she was situated. When, finally, she was bidden write down her visions, at once all her maladies left her.

"When, on one occasion, I was very much exhausted by my sickness," says she in her own biography of herself, "I asked the nurse who attended me whether she saw things in any other way than with her eyes; she made me no answer. Then I was frightened, and I dared say no more about it to any one. But sometimes, inadvertently, when I was talking, I let slip prophetic sentences. And when I was, so to say, full of this inner vision, then I spoke much which was quite unintelligible to those about me. And when the force of the ecstasy grew, and I spoke something about it, more after the manner of a child than of a girl of my years, then I blushed and

105

cried, and wished heartily that I had held my tongue. But out of dread of what would be said, I never dared to speak out openly as to what I saw. However (Jutta) the noble lady with whom I was had cognisance of this and consulted a monk of her acquaintance."

To one in this condition, plenty of exercise, wholesome food, and hard work, and her head under the pump if she gave way to her fancies, would have been proper treatment. But in the twelfth century no one had any conception that hysteria was a physical disorder.

Jutta died in 1136, and by unanimous vote of the sisters Hildegarde was elected to be superior of the convent, when aged eight-and-thirty. She had now full opportunity to give way to her desire to take that prominent place to which she felt she was called. Two years, however, elapsed before she had made up her mind to write her visions and prophecies. There were difficulties in her way: she could not write, she knew nothing of grammar, and she was perhaps dubious how the world would accept revelations which were in shockingly bad grammar and spelling, and displayed profound ignorance of the real meaning of Scripture. However, she consulted one of the monks of the monastery of S. Disibod, and he put the matter before the rest.

Now, as she was evidently sincere, and there could be no suspicion that Hildegarde was deceiving them, they had to decide whether these visions were from heaven or from hell. That there was a third alternative never for an instant occurred to them: it could not, in the nature of things, in the then condition of medical science, or rather ignorance. Manifestly there was nothing bad in these revelations, consequently the poor amiable monks were compelled to decide that they came from God.

The difficulty now arose how they were to be published. It was obviously impossible to issue to the world the farrago of grammatic blunders, and the confused nonsense of much that poured from her lips, and so she was given secretaries to write down in decent Latin what they supposed she meant to say. The Archbishop Henry of Mayence was called in before the decisive step was taken. He was an amiable, peace-loving, but feeble man, who was made archbishop in 1142. He gave his verdict in favour of the revelations.

Hildegarde says of herself: "In 1141, when I was forty-two years old and seven months, there came on me a dazzling light from heaven, and flashed through my brains and heart and bosom. It was like a flame that does not burn, but warms, just like a sunbeam. From thenceforth I had the gift of the interpretation of the Scriptures, the Psalms, the Gospels, and the books of the Old and New Testament. I had, however, no understanding of the several

106

words of the text, as to their syllables and cases and tenses. When I have my visions—and I have had them from childhood—I am not asleep, nor feverish, nor am I necessarily in retirement, nor do I see with my bodily eyes, but with those of my soul." Later she wrote: "I am always in a fear and tremble, as I have no certainty within me. But I lift up my hands to heaven, and allow myself to be blown about just like a feather in the wind."

Her first book was called by her Scivias; which was her contraction for Disce vias Domini, "know the ways of the Lord." Probably only the first part of it was sent to the Archbishop of Mayence, who gravely called his clergy into consultation over it. Then, when Pope Eugenius III. came to Treves on his way to the Council of Rheims, he was shown it by the archbishop; he gave it to the Bishop of Verdun and other theologians to be examined. Afterwards, on their report, at the Council in 1148, he read it himself to the bishops there assembled, and it was received with applause.

S. Bernard was present, and he at once saw how much assistance he could get in promoting his darling object, a new crusade, if he could enlist Hildegarde in the cause; and he urged the pope to sanction and bless the prophetess. This Eugenius did in a letter, in which he accorded her his full permission to publish whatever was revealed to her. He could hardly do other. These writings were well intended, purported to do good, and that these visions and prophecies were the mere hallucinations of a diseased mind never could have been supposed at the time.

Hildegarde now shifted her quarters. Troops of women had come to place themselves under her direction, drawn by her fame. She settled on S. Ruprechtsberg, near Bingen, where a suitable convent was erected for her.

But the good monks of S. Disibod asked a favour of her which she could not refuse. They knew next to nothing about their founder, except that he was one of the many Irish who had left their native isle in the fifth century and had spread over Germany and Gaul. Would she through her prophetic power, which looked backwards as well as forwards, write them "by revelation" a life of their founder?

This she accordingly did, and the life she wrote was, she insists, given her "by revelation." It is a long and tedious work, a gush of weak and watery verbiage. When reduced to its elementary constituents, it is found to consist of absolutely nothing more than what was already known—that Disibod came from Ireland, settled on the mount that bore his name afterwards, and died there. But this was distended into a tract of 6,250 words.

Hildegarde's "Natural History" is a very funny book. She did not pretend to derive her knowledge of the property of things from inspiration, but there can be little doubt that, at the time when it was issued, those who regarded her prophecies as infallible, looked also on her enunciation of the properties of natural objects as inspired.

She begins the book by likening the world to a human body: the earth is the flesh, the rocks are the bones, the moisture of the stones is the marrow, the slate rocks are the toe and finger nails, the plants are the hair, and the dew is the perspiration. All plants are either hot or cold; so also are all animals. This is the radical division between them. The recipes given are profoundly silly. For a boil, house-flies are to be taken, their heads cut off, and they are to be arranged like herrings in a barrel round the swelling. A poultice is to cover all—but it is the flies that bring the gathering to a head. Here is one of the shortest of her botanical accounts—that of the meadow convolvulus. "The herb is cold, it has not great powers nor is it of much use. But if a man's nails get scaly and crack, then let him grind up the convolvulus, mix with it a little quicksilver and lay it on his nails, tie a bit of rag round, and his nails will be lovely."

Hildegarde wrote a commentary on the Rule of S. Benedict, another on the Athanasian Creed. She propounded difficult questions in Scripture, and solved them by her inner light, only making the difficulties greater, and always missing the simple meaning of a passage.

S. Hildegarde had her troubles. She did not get on very well with the Archbishops of Mayence. At the instigation of S. Bernard she inflamed the minds of the people with a fever of zeal against the Saracens, and exhorted to a crusade. This resulted in a frightful massacre of Jews at Mayence, instigated by a monk named Badulf. The Archbishop Henry, a mild, amiable man, did what he could to protect the unfortunate Israelites, and opened to them his palace. But a papal legate appeared on the scene, and the Chapter induced him to depose the archbishop. He appealed to Rome, but the cardinals were bribed to declare against him. He had chosen his confidential friend, Arnold of Selnhofen, to take what money he could scrape together to Rome and plead his cause. Arnold made the most solemn assurances of fidelity, and betrayed his trust. He used the money entrusted to him to purchase the deposition of his friend and his own advancement.

The people of Mayence were greatly incensed against Arnold, who was thrust on them by the pope himself, without election by the Chapter, and was invested by the pope the same day on which the friend was degraded whom he had betrayed. On reaching Mayence

Arnold did nothing to appease the popular resentment; his court was magnificent, his servants were splendidly liveried, and his table was noted for its luxury. Knowing what a power Hildegarde was in the diocese, he wrote a hypocritical, canting letter to her, beseeching her prayers. She replied with a sharp admonition: "The living Light saith unto thee, Thou hast a form of zeal only, which I hate. Cleanse restlessness from thy soul, and cease from doing injustice to thy people. Rise up and turn to the Lord, for the time cometh speedily."

Seeing the ferment of men's minds increase, Arnold resolved on leaving Bingen, where he then was, to go into his cathedral city and put down all resistance with a high hand. He purposed lodging the first night in the monastery of S. James, outside the walls. Hildegarde warned him of his danger, but he would not listen. A friend, the abbot of Erbach, also cautioned him. "Bah!" scoffed the archbishop, "these Mainzers are dogs; they bark, but do not bite." When Hildegarde heard this, she said, "The dogs have had their chains broken, and they will tear you to pieces."

He scorned these warnings, and in June 1160 went to the monastery in which he had purposed to lodge. But he had rushed, unwittingly, into the jaws of the lion, for the abbot of S. James was his most deadly enemy. The abbot at once sent tidings to the city that the archbishop was there. A mob poured out of the city gates. The archbishop, hearing the roar of their voices and the tramp of their feet, was paralysed with fear; the rioters entered the abbey, rushed upon him, and a butcher split his head with an axe. The dead body was dragged forth and cast into a ditch, where the peasant women, coming to market, pelted it with rotten eggs and bad cheese.

In 1150 Christian was archbishop, but he was in Italy. He was a man of arms, who loved fighting, and had no relish for the duties of his position. During his absence Hildegarde got into difficulties with the administrator of the see. A certain young man had been buried in the cemetery attached to her monastery who had incurred excommunication. An order was sent her to dig the body up and throw it out of consecrated ground. This she refused to do. She insisted that the young fellow had been absolved and had received the last sacraments, and she furnished a vision in which she had been forbidden to exhume the body. But the administrator did not repose such confidence in her visions as to submit. An interdict was laid on her convent, so that the sisters were forbidden to recite their offices and to have the sacraments administered there.

No priest in the diocese dared disobey, and the whole convent was struck with paralysis. Hildegarde wrote, but could obtain no concession. Then she appealed to the military bishop, who was in

Italy. The administrator sent his account of the affair, and the interdict was renewed. So time passed. Hildegarde still obstinately, and rightly, refused to have the body dug up and cast to the dogs. She wrote again to the archbishop, and finally obtained a removal of the interdict. As she complained, there had been no investigation into the facts—it had been a party move of spite against herself.

Although in 1170 Hildegarde was aged seventy-two, her literary energy did not fail. She still composed treatises, and continued to write letters in answer to those she received, or to thunder against those persons whose conduct deserved reprobation. Her correspondence extended from Bremen and the Netherlands, to Rome, and even to Jerusalem. Her denunciations of abuses, corruptions in the Church, were outspoken, and she even prophesied the fall of the empire and a reformation in religion; but the condition of affairs both in the state and in Christendom were so bad, that it required but little foresight to tell that such could not possibly last without a convulsion.

Her style is not without a certain amount of rude eloquence, but is involved. Those who took down her words were clearly not always able to make out the drift of what she said; but, indeed, she herself probably could not wholly explain them. The words poured forth in a stream, rolling her ideas about in confusion, and she was impatient of her secretaries meddling over-much with her revelations and prophecies, lest they should make sense indeed, but at the expense of their genuine character.

She had one of those eager, restless minds, which at the present day would have made of her a platform oratress, a vehement writer in magazines, and a reformer on school and hospital boards: always vehement with purpose. Her activity, as already said, took several directions—that of exhortation to repentance and good works, that of deep theological research, and of Scriptural interpretation, that also of the study of Natural History. But she did more than that: she wrote hymns and composed melodies. She had never been taught musical science as then understood. That was no loss to her. Her airs are as rambling and incoherent as her prophecies.

She also pretended to speak in an unknown tongue, and to be able to interpret this language. The study of this pretended new language is suggestive and amusing. It has been taken in hand by Grimm, Pitra and Roth. It presents an amusing jumble of words German, Latin, and misunderstood Hebrew.

Hildegarde died at the age of eighty-two, in 1179. She has not been formally canonised; she is, however, inserted as a saint in the Roman kalendar on September 17th, the day of her death.

XVI

S. CLARA

It has been often remarked how that a saint who initiates a reform, or does some great work, has a faithful woman to assist, or carry on his work, and complete it. What he designed for all alike, he was competent only to apply to men, and she carried out his ideas among women. Thus S. Bridget supplemented the achievements of S. Patrick, and S. Hilda those of S. Aidan. Benedict's twin sister Scholastica worked side by side with her brother; and, as we shall now see, S. Clara was the spiritual sister and helpmate of S. Francis. The moon, according to David, is an ever faithful witness in heaven; and yet the moon wanes and for a time disappears. The moon much resembles the Church.

> "The moon above, the Church below,
> A wondrous race they run;
> And all their radiance, all their glow,
> Each borrows from its sun."

As the moon wanes, so there are periods when the Church proves dull, dark, and without much token of spiritual life; but this is for a time only, and precedes a restoration of illumination. The period when S. Francis appeared was one of those of darkness in the Church. The enthusiastic faith of the barbarian kings and nobles, bred of the self-devotion and earnestness of the first missionaries among them, had led to their endowing the Church largely. This was done to enable her to carry on the great work of evangelisation without care for the material concerns of life. But it led to an unfortunate result. As the bishoprics were wealthy, and seats of power, ambitious and greedy men of the noble class rushed into Holy Orders for the sake of these material advantages, and in entire disregard of the religious responsibilities attached to such offices. And as with the prelates, so with the clergy. They seemed to think that the things of Jesus Christ were best served by making themselves comfortable; they were ignorant, careless, and worldly. The great ecclesiastics made a display of their wealth, and exercised their power tyrannically. "The Church might still seem to preach to all," says Dean Milman; "but it preached in a tone of lofty condescension, it dictated rather than persuaded; but, in general, actual preaching had fallen into disuse; it was in theory the special

111

privilege of the bishops, and the bishops were but few who had either the gift, the inclination, or the leisure from their secular, judicial, or warlike occupations to preach even in their cathedral cities; in the rest of their dioceses their presence was but occasional—a progress or visitation of pomp and form, rather than of popular instruction. The only general teaching of the people was the ritual.

"But the splendid ritual, admirably as it was constituted to impress by its words or symbolic forms the leading truths of Christianity upon the more intelligent, or in a vague way upon the more rude and uneducated, could be administered, and was administered, by a priesthood almost entirely ignorant, but which had learned mechanically, not without decency, perhaps not without devotion, to go through the stated observances. Everywhere the bell summoned to the frequent service, the service was performed, and the obedient flock gathered to the chapel or the church, knelt, and either performed their orisons or heard the customary chant and prayer. This, the only instruction which the mass of the priesthood could convey, might for a time be sufficient to maintain in the minds of the people a quiescent and submissive faith, nevertheless, in itself, could not but awaken in some a desire of knowledge, which it could not satisfy.... And just at this time the popular mind throughout Christendom seemed to demand instruction. There was a wide and vague awakening and yearning of the human intellect. Here that which was heresy stepped in and seized upon the vacant mind. Preaching in public and in private was the strength of all the heresiarchs, of all the sects. Eloquence, popular eloquence, became a new power which the Church had comparatively neglected or disdained, since the time of the Crusades. The Patropassians, the Henricians, the followers of Peter Waldo, and the wilder teachers at least, tinged with the old Manichæan tenets of the East, met on this common ground. They were poor and popular; they felt with the people, whether the lower burghers of the cities, the lower vassals, or even the peasants and serfs; they spoke the language of the people, they were of the people. All these sects were bound together by their common aversion to the clergy—not only the wealthy, worldly, immoral, tyrannical, but the decent yet inert priesthood, who left the uninstructed souls of men to perish."[9]

It was when, apparently, the bulk of the population was hesitating whether to break away from the Church, and when certain ardent spirits began to question whether the Church could

---

[9] Latin Christianity, 1867, vol. vi., pp. 1 seq.

be the Kingdom of God, wherein appeared so much of evil, that almost simultaneously two men stood forth to arrest the evil. The story was told afterwards that the pope in a dream had seen the Church under the form of a building tottering to its fall, but that two men rushed forward and sustained it. These men were Dominic and Francis. The former founded an order of preachers, by which Christendom in the West was overspread with a host of zealous, active, and devoted men, whose function was popular instruction.

Francis, seeing the universal greed after lands and money, took the vow of poverty, made that a capital point in his institution. The grasping after possessions should never curse his society, and he donned, and made his disciples don, the poor, coarse dress of the common labourer, to show that they were to be ever of the people, and for the people, even for the lowest. And he aimed first of all to encourage piety—the striving of the soul after God—and to show that within the Church that flame could burn brightest and give out most heat. But he taught as well. It was due to his great desire to bring home to the people the truth of the Incarnation, that he devised the crèche of Christmas, and composed the first Christmas carols. And he was a preacher—fervent, inspired, convincing. His heart so overflowed with love, that even birds and beasts were attracted to him, and his love extended to them—"his sisters and brothers," as he termed them.

The story of the conversion of S. Francis, the wealthy merchant's son, is well known. He was a young man, just at the age when the deepest feelings of man's nature begin to make themselves articulate. One evening he was revelling with his companions of the same age with himself. When supper was over, the merry party dashed out of the hot, lighted room into the open air. The dark indigo-blue vault of heaven overhead was besprent with myriads of stars, and Francis suddenly halted, looked up, and remained silent in contemplation of this wondrous canopy.

"What ails you, Francis?" asked one of the revellers.

"He is star-gazing for a wife," joked another.

"Ah!" said Francis gravely, "for a wife past all that your imagination can conceive."

His soul with inarticulate cravings strained after something higher than a merchant's life behind a counter, a nobler life than revelling and drunkenness. Then probably he first conceived the idea of embracing poverty, and of devoting his whole life to his poor brothers.

The first great gathering of the Order he founded was in 1212, and that same year saw the establishment of a sisterhood in connection with the Society. It came about thus:—

Favorino Scefi was a man of noble family in Assisi, given to the profession of arms, and a good swordsman; his wife, Hortulana, had presented him with three daughters, Clara, Agnes, and Beatrix, but no son.

One day—it was Palm Sunday—in the before-mentioned year, when Clara was aged eighteen, she and her mother were present when Francis preached. The effect of his sermon on her young heart was overwhelming and ineradicable. From this moment she resolved to leave the world and its splendours, and the prospect of marriage, and to devote her whole life to God and to the advancement of His kingdom.

What she was to do, what God's designs were, all was dark before her; only in her was the intense longing to place herself in His hands, that He might use her as He saw fit. And it appeared to her that her desire had been known and her self-offering accepted. As already said, it was Palm Sunday, and the custom was for the bishop to bless the palms that were presented him by the deacon, and to distribute them among those who came up in single file to the altar steps. Clara, shy and retiring, hung back. The bishop's eye rested on her. All at once he stepped down into the nave, the acolytes bearing their tapers before him, and carrying a palm branch, he placed it in the hands of the shrinking maiden.

To her it was as a consecration.

In the evening she ran to the chapel of the Portiuncula, where Francis and his disciples were installed; she fell on her knees and implored to be received, and given work to do. In a paroxysm of devotion she plucked off her little ornaments, and tore away her rich dress.

Francis, unable as he was unwilling to refuse her offer of herself, cast over her a coarse habit, and she was enrolled in the ranks of the Champions of Poverty.

But where was the young girl to be put? He had no other female adherents. He accordingly took her to the Benedictine nunnery of S. Paolo, where she was to remain till he had considered what to do with her.

The parents of Clara were indignant and annoyed when they learned what she had done, and they endeavoured by every means to induce to return to them. They even employed violence. She escaped from them to the altar, and laid hold of the cloth that covered it. They tried to drag her away, but she clung with such tenacity as to tear the very cloth to which she clung.

Clara now removed to another convent of Benedictins, S. Angelo di Panso, where she spent a fortnight in prayer and silence, considering the step she had taken.

114

At the end of that time her sister Agnes, two years younger than herself, came and entreated to be allowed to remain with her. The father was very angry, and called the members of the family together to consult on the matter. Nothing, however, could be done; the two girls were resolute.

In the meantime S. Francis was busy preparing a dwelling for them near a little church of S. Damian that he had restored. When this was complete he removed them to it. Many girls and even women now joined the sisters, and constituted a little community. Francis was appealed to for a rule by which they might form their lives, but this he was unwilling to give. Let them, said he, take Clara herself as their example.

Presently, little Beatrix arrived. She could not bear to be alone in the now desolate home, she yearned to be with her sisters. She also was accepted. After the death of her husband Hortulana also joined them, so that mother and daughters were united again.

As the fundamental rule of Francis was absolute poverty, his brothers were obliged to beg their bread. They went round the town and country with sacks, asking for scraps of food; and as it would not be seemly for the sisters of the house at S. Damian to do the same, the friars were constrained to divide their crusts with them.

Gregory IX very sensibly objected to the friars going in and out of the convent, and he forbade it. "Very well," said Clara; "if holy brothers may not minister to us the Bread of Life, they shall not provide us with the bread that perishes," and she refused the crusts and broken meat they had collected on their rounds. What was to be done? The whole convent would starve. In a few days the Poor Clares would be dead. An express was sent to the Pope. Gregory could defy an emperor, and that such an one as Frederick Barbarossa; but he was no match for an obstinate woman. He gave way.

The rule imposed on the sisterhood by S. Clara was one of dreary penance. Their services in church were to be without music, even on the high festivals. She would not allow those who were ignorant to learn to read, so that to such these services were unintelligible.

In fact, extravagance marked all she did. She did not suffer the sisters ever to interchange a word with each other without permission, and they were all shut up in their convent, which they might not leave. It is true that S. Francis did slightly modify some of this severity. But his own rule of absolute poverty was a mistake. He intended it as a protest against the money and land grabbing which prevailed, not among laymen only, but among ecclesiastics, and also among the monks; but he went too far. He turned his friars into

115

mere beggars. If he had insisted that they should be poor and work for their livelihood, that would have been well; but to employ them as tramps, begging from door to door, and sponging on the honest, hard-working people, was a fatal mistake, and led to very bad results.

So also Clara, in the hope of keeping her sisters devoted only to the service of God, dissuaded, nay, forbade, reading. In place of cultivating the intellect—a splendid gift of God—she made those under her direction bury their talents.

Insensibly, the Manichæan heresy had penetrated all minds, and made men and women think that the body was evil and must be tortured and bullied, and all that was human trampled underfoot, that the soul alone should be cared for. The result was the production of hysterical, ecstatic beings, who were helpless to do anything for themselves, and were, so far as their minds went, idiots.

S. Clara's work would have been worse than useless, positively mischievous, had it not been for one thing. S. Francis, in order to extend religion among the people, had instituted a third branch of his institution, of which the second was that of the Poor Clares. This third order comprised men and women living in the world—in fact, a great guild of pious people, observing very simple rules, which bound all together in the service of God, His Church, and the poor and sick. This spread like wildfire: everywhere men and women, husbands and wives, young men and girls, rich and poor, nobles and merchants, day-labourers and needlewomen, joined this community, encouraged each other in good works, and learned, by knowing each other, to lose class exclusiveness.

Inevitably the charge of the female members of the third order devolved on the Poor Clares. Then other duties sprang up. There were plenty of little orphan girls adrift; these had to be cared for, and the Clares took charge of them. The devout desired to have their daughters taught by them, and they were constrained to open schools,—and thus to cultivate their own minds, and abandon the rule of silence, or at least to modify it. Consequently the order of Poor Clares did a great deal of good, but not in the way in which S. Clara desired.

The time was one of furious intestinal war in Italy between the factions of Guelph and Ghibelline, and there were far more women than men, as the latter had fallen. Children were left without fathers, wives lost their husbands, girls were deprived of their natural protectors, and the convent served as an asylum for these unfortunates, who otherwise would have succumbed.

In 1220 occurred a scene bearing some resemblance to that of

116

the last meeting of S. Benedict and his sister. S. Clara felt a great desire to be with S. Francis and to eat with him; but he constantly refused. At length his companions, seeing how this troubled her, said to him, "Father, it seems to us that this sternness is not in accordance with Christian charity. Pay attention to Clara, and consent to her request. It is but a small thing that she desires of you—just to eat with her. Remember how that, at your preaching, she forsook all that the world offers."

S. Francis answered, "As it is so in your eyes, so let it be. Let the feast be held at the Church of the Portiuncula, for it was in that that she took the vows."

When the appointed day arrived, S. Clara went forth from her convent with one companion, and came to the place appointed, and waited till Francis should arrive. After awhile he appeared, and he caused their common meal to be prepared on the grass. He seated himself beside Clara, and one of his friars beside the nun who had attended S. Clara. Then all the rest of the company gathered about them.

During the first course S. Francis spoke of God so sweetly, so tenderly, that all were rapt in ecstasy, and forgetting their food, remained wondering and thinking only of God.

When the repast was ended, Clara returned to San Damiani greatly comforted. This was her only meeting, for other purposes than those of ghostly counsel, with her friend and father.

S. Francis died in 1226, six years after the meeting; but Clara lived on for more than a quarter of a century after his decease.

Concerning the austerities practised by S. Clara it is unnecessary to write: a knowledge of them would provoke disgust; but they have probably been vastly exaggerated, for had they been what is represented, she could not have lived forty-two years of self-torture. As she died she was heard murmuring that she saw our Lord surrounded with virgins crowned with flowers, and that one, whose wreath was "like a windowed censer," bowed over her and kissed her.

She died in 1257.

We cannot say of S. Clara that she originated a great work of utility. She supplemented the undertaking of S. Francis, and carried his extravagances to a further extreme. But she was sincere, she held to her purpose; and although her foundation was one void of common-sense and right principles, yet, because well intended, it worked itself into one of utility, and continues to the present day in the Latin Communion doing good service.

XVII

S. THERESA

The most beautiful and pathetic female figure that stands out in the age of the great convulsion which rent Europe into two religious camps, is that of Theresa of Avila: beautiful, because of her exquisitely pure and sincere character and strength of purpose; pathetic, because all her saintliness, all her energies, were directed in a false channel, and to build up what crumbled to pieces almost as soon as the breath left her body.

S. Theresa was born at Avila, in Spain, in the province of the same name and the kingdom of Castile, 1515. Her parents belonged to the class of gentry, and were well connected, but not wealthy.

"To know Avila," says Miss G. C. Graham, in her book Santa Teresa, "to wander through its streets, to watch the sun rise and set over the sombre moorlands beyond the city walls—is greatly to know Teresa. In one of its fortress-houses, where on the shield over the gateway the bucklers of the Davilas were quartered with the rampant lion of the Cepedas, she was born and passed her childhood. In the cathedral which looms over the city walls, half church, half fortress, she worshipped and gazed with ardent eyes, and with a thrill of wonder and terror, into the dim mysteries of its roof. In the quiet cloisters of the Encarnacion she passed the greater part of her life of peace and contemplation. These time-stained stones, these silent cloisters—all that remains in outward bodily form of that strangely complex age, which produced her and the gentle San Juan de la Cruz, so different from her in character and tendencies, together with Philip II., the gloomy and conscientious bigot who championed both—shaped and moulded her existence, shut in and controlled her life. Most meet background for her whose whole life was to be one long battle, this city of warriors and knights—their very memory all shadowy."

Her father was twice married, and Theresa was the eldest daughter by the second wife, who bore him seven sons and two daughters. By his first wife he had two sons and a daughter. She says of this family, "They were all bound to one another by a tender love, and all resembled their parents in virtue except myself."

The young men for the most part went to the "Indies" to carve out fortunes for themselves, but always looked back wistfully and with love to the old home and the dear sisters and parents there. There was much that was grand and full of promise in ancient

118

Spanish life—great domestic attachment, simplicity, integrity, and self-respect, together with a dauntless spirit and a love of adventure. But a fatal darkness came over it. The liberal and democratic institutions of the country were destroyed by the King's ambition of obtaining absolute power; and, worst of all, the Inquisition was suffered to scotch and kill all free intellectual life.

Theresa from an early age was full of vital, intellectual and spiritual energies, but none of these was allowed an outlet. With her extraordinary powers, and with her indomitable will, had her energies been directed to expand in practical good works, she might have transformed the position of her countrywomen.

It was, perhaps, impossible for Theresa to revolutionise the position of women in Spain; the thought of attempting such a thing did not occur to her. So she did the only thing that seemed possible—immure them; that they might not gossip, nor fritter their lives in visiting and entertaining.

To return to her biography.

Her favourite brother, Rodrigo, four years older than herself, was her companion in play. Along with him she pored over an old book of the Lives of the Saints and Martyrs. "When I saw the martyrdom which they had suffered for God," she wrote in after years, "it seemed to me that they had bought the enjoyment of God very cheaply, and I longed to die like them. Together with my brother I discoursed how it would be possible to accomplish this. We agreed to go to the land of the Moors, begging our way for the love of God, there to be beheaded; and it seems to me that the Lord gave us courage even at so tender an age, if we could have discovered a means of accomplishing what we desired. But our parents seemed to us the great obstacle." It is said that the two children actually started, carrying with them provisions for the journey. She was then only six or seven. They got out of the town and on to the bridge, where their uncle, who was jogging into Avila on horseback, saw them, stopped and asked what they were about, and whither going. He at once took them home again.

After her mother's death her father took her to the convent of the Encarnacion. Her elder sister had been married in 1531, and there was no one to look after her at home. In the peaceful retreat of the convent she remained for a year and a half, till, falling ill, she was sent home. A visit she paid during her convalescence to her sister Maria, the wife of a Castilian gentleman who had a country house two days' journey from Avila, determined her vocation. Half-way lived her uncle, Pedro de Cepeda, in an old manor-house. He was a grave, formal gentleman, without wife and children, who attended to his estate, and read only religious books. The young girl stayed the night in his house, and the old man asked her to read aloud to him one of his favourite books of devotion. Out of courtesy she concealed her distaste, and read to him in the evening. She remained there more than one night, probably because not strong enough to proceed upon her journey, and every evening continued the reading. She says: "Although the days I stayed with him were few, such was the effect the words of God I read and heard had on my heart, and the good companionship, that I began to understand the truth—that all was nothing, and that the world was vanity, and that everything ended speedily." She prosecuted her journey after this rest, but her mind was working out the solution of her own destiny. She saw life under a new aspect.

She made up her mind to become a nun, though without any very sincere vocation. Her father gave his consent, and she entered the convent of the Encarnacion as a novice.

The sisterhood was easy-going and numerous. So many men at this period went to the New World, that women abounded, and having nowhere else to go, settled into convents for their convenience, and not for the sake of devotion. "The discipline," says Miss Graham, "was not severe; in its atmosphere of relaxation and secularism, worldly rank was as potent as in this century: no strict, demure sisterhood that of the Encarnacion, where nearly a hundred merry, noisy, squabbling, sometimes hungry and chattering, women made the best of a life forced on them."

It was a convenient, harmless sort of pension for middle-aged ladies who were single; but, of course, not quite suited to young girls without a vocation. The sisters went about, paid visits, received friends, just as in an hotel. All would have been well enough had they been given definite work—the education of poor girls, Sunday-schools, nursing the sick, the care of orphans—but they had nothing to occupy their time or their minds except the choir offices in Latin, which they did not understand.

For a while Theresa fell in with this sort of life, frivolity and religion mixed in equal proportions—frivolity bred of idleness. But it did not satisfy her; it was not what she wanted. She was full of impulse and had a soul desirous of better things. Not for a moment did the thought dawn on her that these good women might be made useful in their generation. A woman is hardly ever an innovator, and the notion of innovation never entered the mind of Theresa. The only course that she could take was to make the enclosure of the nuns strict, and to impose silence on their flow of silly talk. Consequently she brooded on the idea of a reform, and a reform in this direction.

Theresa returned to the Encarnacion after a serious catalyptic attack, on Palm Sunday, 1537. She was then about twenty-two; and twenty-five years of her life were spent within its walls in spiritual and physical troubles, all produced by the same cause—having nothing worthy of her powers to occupy her.

Through all these years this grand woman, full of practical commonsense, with fervent devotion to God in her heart, fired with desire to do something for Him, with a really wonderful tact and charm of manner that was irresistible, had been chafing at her impotence.

Talking with a friend one day, she heard that certain nuns of the Carmelite Order, to which the Encarnacion belonged, had gone back to observance of the primitive rule. What that primitive rule was she did not know; but the friend, a widow lady, said: "How should you like to join me, and become barefooted nuns, and help me to found a convent of this sort?" The idea fired the brain of Theresa, and she went to the Superior to ask permission to start a convent of the strict rule. The Superior and Provincial gave their consent after great hesitation, and arranged that the new house should contain thirteen nuns, and enjoy a fixed revenue. But here S. Theresa interposed; she positively refused to have a revenue. The house must be founded in absolute poverty.

"As soon as our intention began to get wind in the town, there arose such a storm of persecution as is quite indescribable. The scoffs, the jeers, the laughter, the outcries that this was a ridiculous, fantastic undertaking, were more than I can speak of."

The Provincial, thinking it would not do to run counter to popular opinion, changed his mind, and refused to permit the foundation.

"In the meantime I was in very bad odour in the house where I was, because I wished to draw the enclosure more tight. The sisters said that I insulted them, and that God was served well in their convent, and that it would be far better for me to devote my energies to procuring money for that house already existing than to found a new one. Some even wanted to put me in prison, and there were but few who took my part."

After about six months she persuaded her sister with great secrecy to buy her a house in Avila. Then, delighted to have a mystery to play with, she set to work to prepare for turning this house into a convent of barefooted Carmelites. Happily for her she obtained the favour of the bishop, and also a papal brief; and then very secretly, on S. Bartholomew's Day, 1562, she and a few intimates moved into this house. All went on smoothly till after dinner. Theresa had lain down for her siesta, when the house was disturbed by the arrival of a messenger from the convent of the

121

Encarnacion with peremptory orders for her return as well as that of two of the nuns she had persuaded to follow her. The convent was in wild excitement. She was obliged to return, but she was able to hold her own; she had the papal brief to display.

What follows is comical. The town council and the cathedral chapter were convulsed at the news. The mayor sent messages about to convoke a grand assembly of the city council to decide what was to be done, and orders to Theresa to leave the house. But she was resolute. Then, when the town council was baffled, the mayor endeavoured to effect a compromise, being much put out at a woman having defied all the city magnates. But she flourished in his face the brief and an authorisation from the bishop, and he returned defeated. The city magnates in high dudgeon appealed to the sovereign, Philip II., and Theresa was obliged also to send a delegate to court to plead her case. The opposition dragged on for a year, but in the end Theresa carried her point. It was not worth the storm in a teacup raised.

This was the beginning. Even in Spain it was felt that a change in monastic life was necessary.

But reform assumed the direction of recurrence to severe asceticism, a phase as out of date as could well be conceived, and which accordingly flickered for a while, and then expired.

Theresa was delighted to enlist some earnest friars in the cause, and they reformed the Carmelite monasteries on the same lines as those she had pursued with the convents.

In her own account of how she founded her various establishments, she says:—

"I lived five years in the convent of S. Joseph at Avila, after I had founded it; and I think that they were the most quiet years of my life. I there enjoyed the tranquillity and calmness which my soul has often since longed for.... The number in the house was thirteen, a number which I was resolved not to exceed. I was much delighted at living among such pure and holy souls, for all their care was to serve and praise our Lord. His Divine Majesty sent us everything necessary without our asking; and whenever we were in want—and that was seldom—their joy was all the greater. I praised the Lord for giving them such heroic virtue, and especially for endowing them with indifference to what concerned their bodies. I, who was their Superior, never remember to have been troubled with any thought in this matter, because I firmly believed that our Lord would not be wanting to those who had no other wish than how to please Him. With regard to the virtue of obedience, I could mention many things which I here saw in them. One at present recurs to me. One day a few cucumbers were given to us, and we were eating them at our meal. The cucumber that fell to my share was rotten inside. I called one of the sisters, and to prove her obedience, bade her plant it in the garden. She asked if she should plant it upright or sideways; I said 'sideways,' and she immediately did so, without the thought occurring to her that it must decay. Her esteem for obedience was so superior to her natural reason, that she acted as if believing that what I ordered was proper."

In course of time, the eager, active mind of Theresa formed a new scheme. She had now a convent of discalced nuns; she was resolved to have also a monastery of discalced friars. The General of her Order came to Avila from Rome; she explained to him the reform she had effected, and her desire to extend the reform to monasteries of men. He acquiesced, and gave her permission to form such a society if she could. "I was now," says she, "much consoled at having his licence, but much troubled at having no friars ready to begin the work, nor any secular ready to start the house. Here was I, a poor barefooted nun, without the support of any one but our Lord, furnished with plenty of letters and good wishes, but without the possibility of putting my wishes into execution."

However, she wrote to the General of the Jesuits at Medina, and he and the rest of the fathers of that Society took the matter up very warmly, and did not desist till they had obtained from the bishop and magistrates licence for the foundation of such a monastery as S. Theresa desired.

"Now, though I had a licence, I had no house, nor a farthing wherewith to buy one; and how could a poor stranger like me procure credit, had not the Lord assisted us? He so ordered that a virtuous lady, for whom there had been no room for admission into S. Joseph's convent, hearing that another house was about to be started, asked to be admitted into it. She had some money, but not enough to buy the house with—only sufficient for the hire of one, and to pay our travelling expenses. And so we hired one; and without any other assistance we left Avila, two nuns from S. Joseph's and myself, with four from the relaxed convent of the Incarnation, and our chaplain Julian d'Avila."

They reached Medina del Campo on the eve of the Assumption, 1567, at midnight, and stole on foot with great secrecy to the hired house. "It was a great mercy of God that at such an hour we met no one, though then was the time when the bulls were about to be shut up which were to fight next day. I have no recollection of anything, I was in such a scare and anxiety. Having come to the house, we entered a court, the walls of which were much decayed. The good father who had hired the house was short-sighted, and had not noticed how unfit the place was to be made an abode for the

123

Blessed Sacrament. When I saw the hall I perceived that much rubbish would have to be removed, and the walls to be plastered. The night was far advanced, and we had brought only a few hangings there, I think, which was nothing for the whole length of the hall. I knew not what was to be done, for I saw that this was not a fit place for an altar to be erected in it. However, our Lord was willing that this should be done immediately, for the steward of the lady had in the house several pieces of tapestry and a piece of blue damask, and we were allowed the use of them. When I saw such good furniture, I praised our Lord. But we knew not what to do for nails, and that was not the time when they could be bought. We began to search for some on the walls, and at length procured enough. Then some of the men put up the tapestry whilst we swept the floor; and we made such haste, that when it was daylight the altar was ready, a bell was put up, and immediately mass was said. This was sufficient for taking possession, but we did not rest till the Blessed Sacrament was placed in the tabernacle, and through the chinks of the door opposite the altar we heard mass, having no other place."

When daylight came S. Theresa was aghast to see how ruinous the house was: the hall, which she had hastily converted into a chapel, was so full of cracks that the Blessed Sacrament was exposed to the sight of those who passed in the streets, and she saw that the repairs of the dilapidated mansion would cost money and take time. She was much dispirited, for she began to fear that she had undertaken what she had not the power to carry out—her intention being to make this a convent of nuns, and then to found, if possible, in the same town, a monastery for reformed Carmelite friars.

"In this trouble I passed a great part of the evening, till the Rector of the Society (of Jesus) sent a father to visit me, and he consoled me greatly. I did not tell him all my troubles, but only that which I felt at seeing ourselves in the street. I spoke to him of the necessity of having another house for us, cost what it might, wherein we might dwell till this one was repaired. I recovered courage also at seeing so many people come to us and none of them accuse me of folly, which was a mercy of God, for they would have done quite right to take away from us the Blessed Sacrament. In spite of all the efforts made to obtain another house, none could be found to be let in the old town, and this gave me great anxiety night and day; for though I had appointed men to watch and guard the Blessed Sacrament, yet I was fearful lest they should fall asleep, and so I got up in the night myself to guard it at a window, and by the clear light of the moon I could see it very plainly.

"About eight days after, a merchant, seeing our necessity, and

124

living himself in a very good house, told us we might have the upper part of it, where we might live as in a private house of our own. He also had a large hall with a gilt ceiling, and this he gave us for a church."

Others came forward and assisted, and the upper story of the merchant's house was fitted up for their reception.

Shortly after she began to see her way towards obtaining friars for her reformed Order. There was in Medina an excellent priest, named Antonio de Heredia, who had assisted her greatly. He told her that he desired to enter the Carthusian Order. This did not please Theresa; she entreated him to delay a year the execution of his design, and she then confided to him her plan. He was pleased with it, and to her great delight offered to be the first friar of her reformed society. Shortly after, she met S. John of the Cross, who was also at the time thinking of joining the Carthusians. She intercepted him, and persuaded him to become a discalced Carmelite. "He promised me he would do so if the business did not prove too tedious. When I now saw I had two religious to commence the work with, it seemed to me that the matter was accomplished, although I was not entirely satisfied with the Prior; and thus some delay was caused, as well as by our not having any place for commencing our monastery."

In 1568, the Lady de la Cerda, sister of the Duke of Medina Sidonia, wrote to S. Theresa, offering to found a house of discalced Carmelite nuns in her own town, Malagon. This lady knew Theresa well; it was with her when left a widow that the saint had spent six months. Theresa at once went to Malagon with some of her nuns, and took possession of the house provided for them.

Four or five months after, whilst S. Theresa was talking to a young gentleman of quality, he most unexpectedly offered her a house he possessed in Valladolid, with a vineyard attached to it. She at once accepted the offer. But when she arrived at Valladolid, she found that the place was unhealthy, and altogether unsuitable. Indeed, all the nuns fell ill in it, and they were obliged to move to another house given them by the sister of the Bishop of Avila.

Shortly after this, a young gentleman of Avila hearing that S. Theresa wished to found a monastery of discalced friars, offered her a house he possessed in the little village of Durvello. She accepted it, and then started to see it, with a nun and her chaplain, Father Julian d'Avila.

"Though we set off at daybreak, yet as the place was not much known, no one could direct us; and thus we walked all that day in great trouble, for the sun was very hot, and when we thought we were near the place, we found that we had still a long way to go. I shall never forget the fatigue and wanderings of that day. We arrived at the place just before nightfall, and when we went into the house, we found it was in such a state that we could not possibly spend the night in it, partly because it was filthy, and partly because there were many people about. It had a tolerable hall, two chambers with a garret, and a little kitchen: this was the building we were to use as our friary. I thought that the hall might be turned into a chapel, the garret into a choir for the friars, and the two chambers into a dormitory. My companion could not endure the thought of making a monastery of the place, and said, 'Mother, no soul can possibly endure such a place as this, however great the sanctity. Speak no more about it.' Father Julian did not oppose me when I expressed my intentions, though he was of the same opinion as my companion. We spent the night in the church, though, so great was our fatigue, we stood more in need of sleep than of vigil. Having arrived at Medina, I spoke with Father Antonio, and told him everything. He answered: 'I am ready to live not only in such a house as that which you describe, but even in a pigsty.' Father John of the Cross was of the same mind."

The consent of the bishop and of the provincial of the Order having been obtained, the two fathers went off to the wretched house, and took possession of it on the first or second Sunday in Advent, in 1568.

"The following Lent, as I was going to Toledo, I passed that way, and came on Father Antonio sweeping the door of the church, with his usual cheerful countenance. 'What is this, father?' said I; 'what has become of your dignity?' 'The time in which I received honour was time ill spent,' he answered.

"When I went into the church along with two merchants, friends of mine, who had come with me from Medina, I was astonished to see how the spirit of the Lord reigned there. So many crosses and skulls were there that the merchants could do nothing but weep. Never shall I forget one little cross placed over the holy water stoup, on which was fixed a paper crucifix, and which produced more devotion than one elaborately carved. The garret formed the choir. It was high in the middle, so that they could stand up there to say the Hours; but to enter it they were obliged to stoop low. They had made two little hermitages on each side of the church, so low that they could only sit or lie down in them, filled inside with hay because it was cold. Their heads almost touched the roof. Two little windows commanded the altar, and two stones served them as pillows. Here was also a store of crosses and skulls.

"They went about preaching among the ignorant people of the neighbourhood, and soon gained such a reputation that I was

126

greatly consoled. They went to preach six or eight miles off, through snow and frost, barefoot, for they wore no sandals then; afterwards they were ordered to wear them. When they had done preaching and confessing they returned late to their meal, but with such joy that all their sufferings were not accounted by them. As for food, they had sufficient, for the people of the neighbouring villages provided them with more than they wanted."

We need not follow the Saint through the course of many years, travelling from place to place, never quiet anywhere, always on the move, with a scheme in her head, which she obstinately determined on carrying out in spite of obstacle and opposition.

When the boys were throwing stones at the frogs in a pond, according to the fable, one old toad raised its head above the water and said to the urchins, "What is fun to you is death to us." The unfortunate women whom S. Theresa immured, the unhappy men whom she persuaded to reduce themselves to poverty and imbecility, might have addressed her in the same words. She, herself, was always engaged on carrying her projects into effect;—absolutely useless though they were, nay, worse than useless, for they were positively mischievous. But those confined in her convents were afforded no work to do, no reading to occupy their minds; they were reduced to a condition of stupidity. The brain is given to man and woman to be exercised, the will to be directed; neither to be effaced.

What was the reform to which Theresa devoted all her energies? To induce certain men and women to kick off their shoes. She aimed at restoring the Carmelite Order to the old severity of its rule at a time when everywhere practical, energetic, active men and women were needed to do good work for God and their fellow-men, instead of moping in cells, looking at blank walls, and shivering with cold in compulsory idleness. She deliberately engaged many hundreds of the Lord's servants in the work of burying their talents.

We cannot but admire her enthusiasm and her singleness of purpose, whilst we regret that neither were aright directed. The bishops and magistrates had sense to see that her undertakings were foolish and unprofitable, but she was able to override their opposition, by her strength of purpose and appeal to higher authorities who thought fit to humour her. She was engaged on making one of her many foundations at Burgos in 1582; but was vigorously opposed by the archbishop, who refused to give his licence.

Sick and disgusted, she left Burgos at the end of July 1582, with Anne of S. Bartholomew and Theresa of Jesus, her niece, and went to Palencia, Medina del Campo, and Alba, which latter place she visited at the request of Maria Henriquez, Duchess of Alba, who was anxious to meet with her. There she died. The account of her death we have from the pen of her companion at the time, the Venerable Anne of S. Bartholomew.

"Having arrived on our way at a little village, she found herself, at night, much exhausted, and she said to me, 'My daughter, I feel very weak; you would do me a pleasure if you could procure me something to eat.' I had only some dry figs with me; I gave four reals to a person wherewith to buy eggs at any price, but none were to be procured. Seeing her half dead, and being in this distress, I could not contain my tears. She said to me, with angelic patience, 'Do not afflict yourself, my daughter; God wills it, and I am content. The fig you have given me suffices.' On the morrow we arrived at Alba; our holy mother was so ill that the doctors despaired of her recovery. I was dreadfully troubled to lose her, and especially at her dying at Alba. I was also grieved to think that I must survive her, for I was very fond of her, and she was very tender towards me; her presence was my great consolation.... I was with her for five days at Alba, in the greatest affliction. Two days before her death, when I was alone with her in her cell, she said to me, 'At last, my daughter, the time of my death is come.' These words touched me to the quick; I did not leave her for a moment, but had everything that was needed brought to me.

"Father Antony of Jesus, one of the first Discalced Carmelites, seeing how tired I was, said to me on the morning of her death, 'Go and take a little something or other.' But when I left the room she seemed uneasy, and looked from side to side. The father asked her if she wished me to be recalled. She could not speak, but she made a sign of assent. I therefore returned, and on my re-entering the room, she smiled, and caressed me, drawing me towards her, and placed herself in my arms. I held her thus for fourteen hours, all which time she was in the most exalted meditation, and so full of love for her Saviour, that she seemed as though she could not die soon enough, so greatly did she sigh for His presence. As for me, I felt the most lively pain till I saw the good Lord at the foot of the bed of the saint, in inexpressible majesty accompanied by some saints, ready to conduct her happy soul to heaven. This glorious vision lasted the space of a credo, and entirely resigned me to the will of the Lord. I said, from the bottom of my heart, 'O my God, even though I should wish to retain her on earth, I would resign her at once to Thee!' I had scarcely said these words when she expired."

Ribera gives the following account of her death:—"At nine o'clock on the same evening she received, with great reverence and devotion, the sacrament of Extreme Unction, joining with the nuns in the penitential psalms and litany. Father Antony asked her, a little after, if she wished her body, after her death, to be taken to Avila, or to remain at Alba. She seemed displeased at the question, and only answered, 'Am I to have a will in anything? Will they deny me here a little earth for my body?' All that night she suffered excessive pain. Next day, at seven in the morning, she turned herself on one side, just in the posture in which the blessed Magdalen is commonly drawn by painters. Thus she remained for fourteen hours, holding a crucifix firmly in her hands, so that the nuns could not remove it till after her death. She continued in an ecstasy, with an inflamed countenance, and great composure, like one wholly taken up with internal contemplation. When she was now drawing near her end, one of the nuns, viewing her more attentively, thought she observed in her certain signs that the Saviour was talking to her, and showing her wonderful things. Thus she remained till nine in the evening, when she surrendered her pure soul into the hands of her Creator. She died in the arms of Sister Anne of S. Bartholomew, on October 4th, 1582; but the next day, on account of the reformation of the calendar, was the fifteenth of that month, the day now appointed for the festival. The saint was sixty-seven years old, forty-seven of which she had passed in religion—twenty-seven in the monastery of the Incarnation, and twenty in that of S. Joseph."

Such was the end of this remarkable woman, whose life was so full of energy directed to no better purpose than that of a squirrel in a revolving cage.

That was not her fault; it was due to the age in which she lived and to the paralysing influence of the Inquisition in the land, which allowed no independence of thought or of action.

We have seen the utter helplessness of Spain exhibited in the War with the United States of America. Not a token of ability, not a sign of fresh vigour appeared—only feebleness, degeneracy, helplessness. It is to this that the Inquisition has reduced Spain. It has destroyed the recuperative, vital energy out of the character of the people.

The Latin races seem doomed by God to go down, and His hand is manifestly extended to bless and lead on the great Anglo-Saxon race. But this can only be so long as that race fulfils its high mission, as the civilising force in the world, and it maintains the eternal principles of Freedom, Justice, and Integrity.

XVIII

SISTER DORA

In S. Hildegarde and S. Theresa we have had instances of two women of wonderful energy and talent, yet who achieved nothing of moment, because their powers were not directed into a channel where they might have been of use. S. Hildegarde, indeed, by her letters, threatening, warning, reproving, did a certain amount of good—not much; those misdoers who received her epistles winced and went on in their old courses. Nevertheless, she was a testimony to a worldly age of the higher life set before it in the Gospel than that world cared to follow.

S. Theresa, with a heart on fire with love to God, and inexhaustible energy, spent herself in founding little nunneries, in which the sisters were, as a reform, to wear sandals instead of shoes, and in which their natural gifts were to be reduced to a general level of incapacity, by giving them nothing practical to do, and by forbidding them the cultivation of their intellects.

Sister Dora, whose life I purpose sketching, strikes me as having been a double of S. Theresa, in the same persistency, determined will, fascination of manner, and cheerfulness. Neither could be happy until afforded scope for the exercise of her powers—but how different were the ends set before each!

A very charming biography of Sister Dora has been written by Miss Lonsdale, which, whilst admirably portraying her character, has given some umbrage by painting the people among whom she laboured in darker colours than they conceive is justified, and by a little heightening of the dramatic situations. She fell, moreover, into certain inaccuracies in matters of detail, and some of her statements have been contradicted by persons who were qualified to know particulars. What mistakes were made in that book have in part been corrected in later editions. But I cannot find that there was any accusation made of the authoress unduly idealising the character of Sister Dora. On the contrary, some think that Miss Lonsdale, in her desire not to appear a panegyrist, has given Sister Dora a tincture of unworthy qualities that were really absent from her character.[10]

---

[10] The Rev. E. M. Fitzgerald, who was Vicar of Walsall at the time when Sister Dora was there, writes: "No Walsall friend of Sister Dora ever thought that the book exaggerated her virtues or her achievements. We

130

In compiling this little notice I have taken pains to obtain information from those who knew Sister Dora intimately, and have had Miss Lonsdale's book subjected to revision by such as live in Walsall or knew Walsall when she was there; and I trust that it is free from inaccuracies and exaggerations.

In addition to Miss Lonsdale's Memoir two others appeared, one in Miss J. Chappell's Four Noble Women and their Work, and another by Miss Morton, which has been characterised in the Walsall Observer as a "caricature." Neither of these afford any additional matter of value.

In addition again, but of very different value, is a notice by Mr. S. Welsh, Secretary to the Hospital at Walsall, in which she worked, and who was introduced to her the day after she arrived there, and was on terms of intimacy with her till her death. His notice is in the General Baptist Magazine for 1889. This is the more valuable as being the testimony of one belonging to a different religious communion, and is, therefore, sure to be impartial. Another corrective to mistakes is contained in Sister Dora: a Review, published at Walsall in 1880. I enter into all these particulars at some length because Miss Lonsdale's book was qualified by the Rev. Mark Pattison, Sister Dora's brother, as "a romance," and because some people have considered it to be so, misdoubting the main facts because of the inaccuracies in detail fastened on at the time. Mr. Mark Pattison was unqualified spiritually for entering into and appreciating his sister's character; and of her life in Walsall he personally knew absolutely nothing. A cold and soured man, wrapped up in himself, he could not appreciate the overflowing charity and devotion of his sister.

Dorothy Wyndlow Pattison was born on the 15th January, 1832. She was the youngest daughter, and the youngest child but one, of the Rev. Mark Pattison, who was for many years Rector of Hauxwell, near Richmond, in Yorkshire. She inherited from her father, who was of a Devonshire family, that finely proportioned and graceful figure which she always maintained; and from her mother, who was the daughter of a banker in Richmond, those lovely features which drew forth the admiration of every one who had the pleasure of knowing her.

Her father was a good and sincere man of the Low Church School. He was thoroughly upright and strict. It is not a little painful to see how Mr. Mark Pattison, his son, late Rector of Lincoln College, Oxford, in his Memoirs can hardly mention his father

---

found fault because it did her injustice in attributing to her some mean faults of which she was incapable."

without some acrimonious remark. But in that sour effusion there is little of generous recognition of any one. Even his sister, the subject of this memoir, comes in for ill-natured comment.

Dora and her sisters, like a thousand other country parsons' daughters, were of the utmost use in their father's Yorkshire parish. A French gentleman who had lived a while in England and in the country, said to me one day: "Your young ladies astound me. They are angels of mercy. They wear no distinguishing habit; one does not see their wings, yet they fly everywhere, and everywhere bring grace and love and peace,—in my country such a thing would be impossible."

These Pattison girls were for ever saving their pocket-money to give it away, and they made it a rule to mend and remake their old frocks, so as not to have to buy new ones out of their allowance for clothes, so as to have more to give. Even their dinners they would reserve for poor people, and content themselves with bread and cheese.

"Giving to others, instead of spending on themselves, seems to have been the rule and delight of their lives," says Miss Lonsdale.

A pretty story is told of her at this time. A schoolboy in the village, who was specially attached to her, fell ill of rheumatic fever. The boy's one longing was to see "Miss Dora" again, but she was abroad on the Continent. As he grew worse and worse, he constantly prayed that he might live long enough to see her. On the day on which she was expected, he sat up on his pillows intently listening, and at last, long before any one else could hear a sound of wheels, he exclaimed, "There she is!" and sank back. She went to him at once, and nursed him till he died.

Her beauty was very great: large brilliant brown eyes, full red lips, a firm chin, and a finely cut profile. Her hair dark, and slightly curling, waved all over her head; and the remarkable beauty and delicacy of her colouring and complexion, added to the liveliness of her expression, made her a fascinating creature to behold. Her father always called her "Little Sunshine."

But the most remarkable feature about her was to be found in her inner being. An indomitable will, which no earthly power could subdue, enabled her to accomplish an almost superhuman work; yet at times it was to her a faculty that brought her into difficulties. She was twenty-nine before she was able to find real scope for her energies, and then she took a bold step—answered an advertisement from a clergyman at Little Woolston, in Buckinghamshire, for a lady to take the village school. Her mother had died in 1861, and she considered herself free from duties that bound her to her home. Her father did not relish the step she took, but acquiesced. She went to

Woolston, and remained there three years, during which time she won the hearts, not of the children only, but of their parents as well. She had to live alone in a cottage, and do everything for herself; but the people never for a moment doubted she was a real lady, and always treated her with great respect. Not thinking a little village school sufficient field for her energies, she resolved to join a nursing sisterhood at Redcar, in Yorkshire. It was a foundation made by a clergyman of private means, the Rev. J. Postlethwaite, and there were in it no vows made except one, limited in period, of obedience to the Superior. The life was not quite suited to her with her strong will, but it did her good. She learned there how to make beds and to cook. "At first she literally sat down and cried when the beds that she had just put in order were all pulled to pieces again by some superior authority, who did not approve of the method in which they were made." But it was a useful lesson for her after-life in a hospital. She was there till the early part of 1865, and then was sent to Walsall to help at a small cottage hospital, which had already been established there for more than a year.[11]

Walsall, though not in the "Black Country," is in a busy manufacturing district, chiefly of iron. At the time when Sister Dora went there it contained a population of 35,000 inhabitants. It is now connected with Birmingham, by almost continuous houses and pits and furnaces, with Wednesbury as a link.

As fresh coal and iron pits were being opened in the district round Walsall, accidents became more frequent, and it was found impracticable to send those injured to Birmingham, which was seven miles distant; accordingly, in 1863, the Town Council invited the Redcar Society to start a hospital there. When the Sister who had begun the work fell ill, Sister Dora was sent in her place, and almost directly caught small-pox from the out-patients. She was very ill, and even in her delirium showed the bent of her mind by ripping her sheets into strips to serve as bandages. She was placed in one small room, with a window looking into the street, of which the blinds were drawn. The most absurd rumours got about that this was the Sisters' oratory, where they had set up an image of the Virgin Mary; and stones and mud were thrown at the panes of glass, and the Sisters were shouted after in the streets. The committee of

---

[11] Miss Lonsdale says that when her father was dangerously ill Sister Dora asked leave to go to him, and was refused and sent down into Devonshire. This has been denied, and I think there has been a misapprehension somewhere. Mr. Welsh says: "The story about Sister Dora not being allowed to visit her father on his death-bed is very sensational, but—is fiction."

the hospital were interrogated, and denied that any religious services were conducted in an oratory. Indeed, no formal oratory would have been allowed; but no doubt the committee were unable to prevent the poor Sisters from saying their prayers together in a room if they agreed to do so, and in community life common prayer is a requisite.

A boy who had received an injury was taken to the hospital. One night, when he was recovering, Sister Dora found him crying. She asked him what was the matter. At last it came out: "Sister, I shouted after you in the street, 'Sister of Misery!'"

"I knew you when you came in," she said; "I remembered your face."

This is the true version of a story Miss Lonsdale gives.

Mr. Welsh says: "When the cottage hospital—which was the second of its kind in England—was opened, the system of voluntary nursing was unknown; the only voluntary nurses heard of then being those who had gone out to the Crimea with Miss Florence Nightingale; consequently the dress of the Sisters was uncommon, and the name of Sister strange. Therefore, a good deal of misunderstanding was the result; but in course of time people began to judge the institution by its results. Still, when Sister Dora came to the hospital, there lingered doubts and suspicions that the nurses were Romanists in disguise, come to entrap and ruin souls rather than cure bodies. But Sister Dora, by her frank, open manner, disarmed suspicion, while the sublime eloquence of noble deeds silenced slanderous tongues, put all opposition to shame, and won for the hospital the confidence of the public, and for herself the admiration and affection of the people."

In 1866 she had a serious illness, brought on by exposure to wet and cold. She would come home from dressing wounds in the cottages, wet through and hot with hurrying along the streets, to find a crowd of out-patients awaiting her return at the hospital, and she would attend to them in total disregard of herself, and allow her wet clothes to dry on her.

This neglect occurred once too often; a chill settled on her, and for three weeks she was dangerously ill. Then it was that the people of Walsall began to realise what she was, and the door of the hospital was besieged by poor people come to inquire how their "Sister Dora" was.

At some time previous to her going to Walsall, her faith had been somewhat disturbed by one who ought not to have endeavoured to subvert her trust in Christianity. This gave her inexpressible uneasiness and unhappiness. There seems to have been always in her a keen sense of God's presence, and confidence in the efficacy of prayer. She now went through this terrible inner trial. An unbelieving artisan who was once nursed by her, and had observed her critically and suspiciously, said, when he left, "She is a noble woman; but she would have been that without her Christianity." There he was mistaken. It was precisely her fast hold, which she regained, of Christianity that made her what she was.

Happily she had one now of great assistance to her as a guide—a very remarkable man, the Rev. Richard Twigg, of St. James's, Wednesbury. Every Sunday morning, when able, she walked over to St. James's to Early Communion. She found in Mr. Twigg a man of deep spiritual insight, and with a heart overflowing with the love of God, and consumed with a desire to win souls to Christ. He was a man with the spirit, and some of the power, of an Apostle—a man who left his stamp on Wednesbury, that will not soon be obliterated.

The struggle through which she had passed, the sense of need in her own soul for all that the Christian Church supplies in teaching and in Sacraments had a great strengthening and confirming effect that never left her; and the love of Jesus Christ became an absorbing personal devotion that nothing could shake. It was this—the love of God—that made her what she was, and endure what she did.

Some time after this she became deeply attached to a gentleman who was connected with the hospital, and he was devotedly fond of her, and proposed to her. But he was an unbeliever. Again she had to pass through an agonising struggle. She felt, as Mr. Twigg pointed out, that to unite her destinies with him was to jeopardise her recovered faith, and she was convinced that to be true to her profession, above all true to her Master, she must refuse the offer. She did so, and probably felt in the end that peace of mind which must ensue whenever a great sacrifice has been made for duty.

Miss Lonsdale represented Sister Dora as somewhat domineering over the managing committee of the hospital. But this is incorrect. A Nonconformist minister says: "The noble object (i.e. the hospital) had moved men of every shade of politics, and every form of religious belief, to the work, and there have been passages in its history not pleasant to remember, but not one of these in the remotest degree involved Sister Dora. On the contrary, her presence and counsel always brought light and peace, and lifted every question into a higher sphere. 'Ask Sister Dora,' it used to be said. 'Had we not better send for Sister Dora?' some member would exclaim out of the fog of contention. Thereupon she would appear; and many well remember how calmly self-possessed, and clear-

135

sighted, she would stand—never sit down. Indeed, there were those who worked with her fifteen years who never saw her seated; she would stand, usually with her hand on the back of the chair which had been placed for her, every eye directed to her; nor was it ever many moments before she had grasped the whole question, and given her opinion just as clearly and simply and straight to the purpose as any opinion given to the sufferers in the wards. Nor was she ever wrong; nor did she ever fail of her purpose with the committee. No committee-men ever questioned or differed from Sister Dora, yet in her was the charm of unconsciousness of power or superiority, and the impression left was, of there being no feeling of pleasure in her, other than the triumph of the right."[12]

In 1867 the cottage hospital had to be abandoned, as erysipelas broke out and would not be expelled. The wards were evidently impregnated with malignant germs, to such an extent that the committee resolved to build a new hospital in a better situation.

"Sister Dora's work became more engrossing when this larger field was opened for it; the men's beds were constantly full, and even the women's ward was hardly ever entirely empty."

Just at this period an epidemic of small-pox broke out in Walsall, and all the energies of Sister Dora were called into play. She visited the cottages where the patients lay, and nursed them or saw to their being supplied with what they needed; whilst at the same time carrying on her usual work at the hospital.

"One night she was sent for by a poor man who was dying of what she called 'black-pox,' a violent form of small-pox. She went at once, and found him in the last extremity. All his relations had fled, and a neighbour alone was with him. When Sister Dora found that only one small piece of candle was left in the house, she gave the woman some money, begging her to go and buy some means of light whilst she stayed with the man. She sat on by his bed, but the woman, who had probably spent the money at the public-house, never returned; and after some little while the dying man raised himself up in bed with a last effort, saying, 'Sister, kiss me before I die.' She took him, all covered as he was with the loathsome disease, into her arms and kissed him, the candle going out almost as she did so, leaving them in total darkness. He implored her not to leave him while he lived, although he might have known she would never do that." So she sat through the night, till the early dawn breaking in revealed that the man was dead.

When the bell at the head of her bed rang at night she rose at once, saying to herself, "The Master is come, and calleth for thee!"

---

[12] Sister Dora: a Review, p. 14 (Walsall, 1880).

136

Indeed, she loved to think that she was ministering to her Blessed Lord in the person of His poor and sick. Miss Lonsdale prints a letter from a former patient in the hospital, from which only a short extract can be made: "I had not been there above a week when Sister Dora found me a little bell, as there was not one to my bed, and she said, 'Enoch, you must ring this bell when you want Sister.' This little bell did not have much rest, for whenever I heard her step or the tinkle of her keys in the hall I used to ring my bell, and she would call out, 'I'm coming, Enoch,' which she did, and would say, 'What do you want?' I often used to say, 'I don't know, Sister,' not really knowing what I did want. She'd say, 'Do you want your pillows shaking up, or do you want moving a little?' which she'd do, whatever it was, and say, 'Do you feel quite cosy now?' 'Yes, Sister.' Then she would start to go into the other ward, but very often before she could get through the door I'd call her back and say my pillow wasn't quite right, or that my leg wanted moving a little. She would come and do it, whatever it was, and say, 'Will that do?' 'Yes, Sister.' Then she'd go about her work, but at the very next sound of her step my bell would ring, and as often as my bell rang Sister would come; and some of the other patients would often remark that I should wear that little bell out or Sister, and she'd say, 'Never mind, for I like to hear it, and it's never too often.' And it rang so often that I've heard Sister say that she often dreamt she heard my little bell and started up in a hurry to find it was a dream."

Sister Dora said once to a friend, who was engaging a servant for the hospital, "Tell her this is not an ordinary house, or even a hospital. I want her to understand that all who serve here, in whatever capacity, ought to have one rule, love for God, and then, I need not say, love for their work."

She spoke often, and with intense earnestness, on the duty, the necessity, of prayer. It was literally true that she never touched a wound without raising her heart to God and entreating Him to bless the means employed. As years glided away, she became able almost to fulfil the Apostle's command: "Pray without ceasing." And her prayers were animated by the most intense faith—an absolutely unshaken conviction of their efficacy. It may truly be said that those who pray become increasingly more sure of the value of prayer. They find that, whatever men may say about the reign of law and the order of Nature, earnest prayer does bring an answer, often in a marvellous manner. The praying man or woman is never shaken in his or her trust in the efficacy of prayer. "She firmly held to the supernatural power, put into the hands of men by means of the weapon of prayer; and the practical faithlessness in this respect of

137

the world at large was an ever-increasing source of surprise and distress to her."

Since her death, in commemoration of her labours at Walsall, a very beautiful statue has been there erected to her, and on the pedestal are bas-reliefs representing incidents in her life there. One of these illustrates a terrible explosion that took place in the Birchett's Iron Works, on Friday, October 15th, 1875, whereby eleven men were so severely burnt that only two survived. All the others died after their admission into the hospital. It came about thus. The men were at work when water escaped from the "twyer" and fell upon the molten iron in the furnace and was at once resolved into steam that blew out the front of the furnace, and also the molten iron, which fell upon the men. Some suffered frightful agonies, but the shock to the nervous system of others had stupefied them. The sight and the smell were terrible. Ladies who volunteered their help could not endure it, and were forced to withdraw, some not getting beyond the door of the ward. But Sister Dora was with the patients incessantly till they died, giving them water, bandaging their wounds, or cutting away the sodden clothes that adhered to the burnt flesh. Some lingered on for ten days, but in all this time she never deserted the fetid atmosphere of the ward, never went to bed.

She had so much to do with burns that she became specially skilful in treating them. Children terribly burnt or scalded were constantly brought to the hospital; often men came scalded from a boiler, or by molten metal. She dressed their wounds herself, but, if possible, always sent the patients to be tended at home, where she would visit them and regularly dress their wounds, rather than have the wards tainted by the effluvium from the burns. Her treatment of burnt children merits quotation.

"If a large surface of the body was burnt, or if the child seemed beside itself with terror, she did not touch the wounds themselves, but only carefully excluded the air from them by means of cotton wool and blankets wrapped round the body. She put hot bottles and flannel to the feet, and, if necessary, ice to the head. Then she gave her attention to soothing and consoling the shocked nerves—a state which she considered to be often a more immediate source of danger to the life of the child than the actual injuries. She fed it with milk and brandy, unless it violently refused food, when she would let it alone until it came round, saying that force, or anything which involved even a slight further shock to the system, was worse than useless. Sometimes, of course, the fatal sleep of exhaustion, from which there was no awakening, would follow; but more often than not food was successfully administered, and after a

138

few hours, Sister Dora, having gained the child's confidence, could dress the wounds without fear of exciting the frantic terror which would have been the result of touching them at first."

Children Sister Dora dearly loved; her heart went out to them with infinite tenderness, and she was even known to sleep with a burnt baby on each arm. What that means only those know who have had experience of the sickening smell arising from burns.

Once a little girl of nine was brought into the hospital so badly burnt that it was obvious she had not many hours to live. Sister Dora sat by her bed talking to her of Jesus Christ and His love for little children, and of the blessed home into which He would receive them. The child died peacefully, and her last words were: "Sister, when you come to heaven, I'll meet you at the gates with a bunch of flowers."

One of the most heroic of her many heroic acts was taking charge of the small-pox hospital when a second epidemic broke out.

Mr. S. Welsh says:—"In the spring of 1875 there was a second visitation of the disease, and fears were entertained that the results would be as bad as during the former visitation. One morning Sister Dora came to me and said, 'Do you know, I have an idea that if some one could be got to go to the epidemic hospital in whom the people have confidence, they would send their friends to be nursed, the patients would be isolated, and the disease stamped out?'" This was because a prejudice was entertained against the new small-pox hospital, and those who had sick concealed the fact rather than send them to it. "I said," continues Mr. Welsh, "'I have long been of the opinion you have just expressed; but where are we to get a lady, in whom the people would have confidence, to undertake the duty?' Her prompt reply was, 'I will go.' I confess the sudden announcement of her determination rather took me by surprise, for I had no expectation of it, and not the most remote idea that she intended to go. 'But,' I said, 'who will take charge of the hospital if you go there?' 'Oh,' she replied, 'I can get plenty of ladies to come there, but none will go to the epidemic. And,' she added, by way of reconciling me to her view, 'it will only be for a short time.' 'But what if you were to take the disease and die?' I inquired. 'Then,' she added, in her cheery way, 'I shall have died in the path of duty, and, you know, I could not die better.' I knew it was no use pointing out at length the risk she ran, for where it was a case of saving others, self with her was no consideration. I tried to dissuade her on other grounds.... A few days later, I was in company with the doctor of our hospital, who was also medical officer of health, and who, as such, had charge of the epidemic hospital, near to which we were at the time. He said, 'Do you know where Sister Dora is?' 'At the hospital, I suppose,' was my reply. 'No,' he rejoined, 'she is over there!'—pointing to the epidemic hospital.... The people, as soon as they knew Sister Dora was in charge, had no misgiving about sending their relatives to be nursed, and the result was as she had predicted; the cases were brought in as soon as it was discovered that patients had the disease, and the epidemic was speedily stamped out."

She had, however, a hard time of it there, as she lacked assistants. Two women were sent from the workhouse, but they proved of little use. The porter, an old soldier, was attentive and kind in his way, but he always went out "on a spree" on Saturday nights, and did not return till late on Sunday evening. When the workhouse women failed her, she was sometimes alone with her patients, and these occasionally in the delirium of small-pox.

It was not till the middle of August, 1875, that the last small-pox patient departed from the hospital, and she was able to return to her original work.

One of the bas-reliefs on her monument represents Sister Dora consoling the afflicted and the scene depicted refers to a dreadful colliery accident that occurred on March 14th, 1872, at Pelsall, a village rather over three miles from Walsall, by which twenty-two men were entombed, and all perished. For several days hopes were entertained that some of the men would be got out alive; and blankets in which to wrap them, and restoratives, were provided, and Sister Dora was sent for to attend the men when brought to "bank." The following extract, from an article by a special correspondent in a newspaper, dated December 10th, 1872, will give some idea of Sister Dora's connection with the event:—

"Out of doors the scene is weird and awful, and impresses the mind with a peculiar gloom; for the intensity of the darkness is heightened by the shades created by the artificial lights. Every object, the most minute, stands out in bold relief against the inky darkness which surrounds the landscape. On the crest of the mound or pit-bank, the policemen, like sentinels, are walking their rounds. The wind is howling and whistling through the trees which form a background to the pit-bank, and the rain is coming hissing down in sheets. In a hovel close to the pit-shaft sit the bereaved and disconsolate mourners, hoping against hope, and watching for those who will never return. There, too, are the swarthy sons of toil who have just returned from their fruitless search in the mine for the dear missing ones, and are resting while their saturated clothes are drying. But another form glides softly from that hovel; and amid the pelting rain, and over the rough pit-bank, and through miry clay—now ankle deep—takes her course to the dwellings of the mourners, for some, spent with watching, have been induced to return to their

140

homes. As she plods her way amid pieces of timber, upturned waggons, and fragments of broken machinery, which are scattered about in great confusion, a 'wee, wee bairn' creeps gently to her side, and grasping her hand, and looking wistfully into her face, which is radiant with kindness and affection, says, 'Oh, Sister, do see to my father when they bring him up the pit.' Poor child! Never again would he know a father's love, or share a father's care. She smiled, and that smile seemed to lighten the child's load of grief, and her promise to see to his father appeared to impart consolation to his heavy, despairing heart.

"On she glides, with a kind word or a sympathetic expression to all. One woman, after listening to her comforting words, burst into tears—the fountains of sorrow so long pent up seemed to have found vent. 'Let her weep,' said a relative of the unfortunate woman; 'it is the first tear she has shed since the accident has occurred, and it will do her good to cry.' But who is the good Samaritan? She is the sister who for seven years has had the management of the nursing department in the cottage hospital at Walsall."

This is written in too much of the "special correspondent" style to be pleasant; nevertheless it describes what actually took place.

Mr. Samuel Welsh says: "I remember one evening I was in the hospital when a poor man who had been dreadfully crushed in a pit was brought in. One of his legs was so fearfully injured that it was thought it would be necessary to amputate it. After examining the patient, the doctor came to me in the committee-room—one door of which opened into the passage leading to the wards, and another into the hall in the domestic portion of the building. After telling me about the patient who had just been brought in, he said, 'Do you know Sister Dora is very ill? So ill,' he continued, 'that I question if she will pull through this time.' I naturally inquired what she was suffering from, and in reply the doctor said, 'She will not take care of herself, and is suffering from blood-poison.' He left me, and I was just trying to solve the problem—— 'What shall be done? or how shall her place be supplied if she be taken from us by death?' when I saw a spectral-like figure gliding gently and almost noiselessly through the room from the domestic entrance to the door leading to the wards. The figure was rather indistinct, for it was nearly dark; and as I gazed at the receding form, I said, 'Sister, is it you?' 'Whist!' she said, and glided through the doorway into the wards. In a short time she returned, and I said to her, 'Sister, the doctor has just been telling me how ill you are—how is it you are here?' 'Ah!' replied she, 'it is true I am very ill; but I heard the surgeons talking about amputating that poor fellow's limb, and I wanted to see whether or

141

no there was a possibility of saving it, and I believe there is; and, knowing that, I shall rest better.' So saying, she glided as noiselessly out of the room as when she entered.

"On her recovery—which was retarded by her neglecting herself to attend to others—she called me to the hall-door of the hospital, and asked me if I thought it was going to rain. I told her I did not think it would rain for some hours. She then told me to go and order a cab to be ready at the hospital in half an hour. I tried to persuade her not to venture out so soon; but it was no use—she went; and many a time I wondered where she went to.

"About six months afterwards I happened to be at a railway station, and saw a pointsman who had been in our hospital with an injured foot, but who, as his friends wished to have him at home, had left before his foot was cured. I inquired how his foot was. He replied that had it not been for Sister Dora he would have lost his foot, if not his life. I said, 'How did she save your foot when you were not in the hospital, and she was ill at the time you left the hospital?' 'Well,' he replied, 'you know my foot was far from well when I left the hospital; there was no one at our house who could see to it properly, and it took bad ways, and one evening I was in awful pain. Oh, how I did wish for Sister Dora to come and dress it! I felt sure she could give me relief, but I had been told she was very ill, so I had no hope that my earnest desire would be realised; but while I was thinking and wishing, the bedroom door was gently opened, and a figure just like Sister Dora glided so softly into the room that I could not hear her, but oh! she was so pale that I began to think it must be her spirit; but when she folded the bedclothes from off my foot, I knew it was she. She dressed my foot, and from that hour it began to improve.'

"A few days after this interview with the pointsman I was talking to Sister Dora and said, 'By the bye, Sister, I have found out where you went with the cab that day.' She replied with a merry twinkle in her eye, 'What a long time you have been finding it out!'"

Her old patients ever remembered her with gratitude. A man called Chell, an engine-stoker, was twice in the hospital under her care, first with a dislocated ankle, severely cut; the second time, with a leg crushed to pieces in a railway accident. It was amputated. According to his own account he remembered nothing of the operation, except that Sister Dora was there, and that, "When I come to after the chloroform, she was on her knees by my side with her arm supporting my head, and she was repeating:—

"'They climbed the steep ascent of heaven,
Through peril, toil, and pain:

142

O God, to us may grace be given
To follow in their train.'

And all through the pain and trouble that I had afterwards, I never forgot Sister's voice saying those words." When she was in the small-pox hospital, avoided by most, this man never failed to stump away to it to see her and inquire how she was getting on.

There were, as she herself recognised, faults in the character of Sister Dora; and yet, without these faults, problematical as it may seem, it is doubtful whether she could have achieved all she did.

One who knew her long and intimately writes to me: "A majestic character, brimming over with sympathy, but, for lack of self-discipline, this sympathy was impulsive and gushing. Her character would have been best formed in marrying a man—either statesman, philanthropist or author—whose character would have dominated hers, and she would have shone subdued. Her glorious nature, physical and mental, was marred by undisciplined impulse. Her nature found its congenial outlet in devoted works of mercy and love to her fellow-creatures. How far she would have done the same under authority, I fear is a little doubtful."

I doubt it wholly. "The wind bloweth where it listeth, and thou hearest the sound thereof, but canst not tell whence it cometh, and whither it goeth: so is every one that is born of the Spirit" (John iii 8). The truth and depth of these words are not sufficiently appreciated. They teach that in those governed by the Spirit of God there is an apparent capriciousness and impulsiveness which does not commend itself to worldly wisdom or vulgar common-sense. Unquestionably, in community life, this masterfulness in the character of Sister Dora might have been subdued, but—would she have then done the same magnificent work? It seems to me—but I may be mistaken—that we should suffer these strong characters to take their course, and not endeavour to crush them into an ordinary mould. It is precisely those who soar above the routine-bound souls that, among men, make history—as Cæsar, Napoleon, Bismarck—and let me add Lord Kitchener. And in the Church it is the same.

Miss Twigg, who knew her well, writes me: "She was a lovable woman, so bright and winsome. She used to come into our rather dull and sad home (our mother died when we were quite children) after evening service. She would nurse one of us, big as we were then, and the others would gather round her, while she would tell us stories of her hospital life.... She was a real woman, though with a woman's failings."

There is one point in Sister Dora's life to which sufficient attention has not been paid by her biographers. It is one which the busy workers of the present day think of too little—namely, the writing of bright, helpful letters to any friend who is sick, or in trouble. Somehow or other she always found time for that, wrote one who knew her well,[13] and who contributes the following, written to a young girl who was at the time in a spinal hospital, and who was almost a stranger to her:—

"My dear Miss J.,—I was so glad to hear from you, though I fear it must be a trouble for you to write. I do hope that you will really have benefited by the treatment and rest. I am so glad that the doctor is good to his 'children.' Such little attentions when you are sick help to alleviate wonderfully. I wish I could come and take a peep at you. Did Mrs. N. tell you that she had sent us £5 for our seaside expedition? Was it not good of her? Oh! we shall have such a jolly time. To see all those poor creatures drink in the sea-breezes! We have had a very busy week of accidents and operations. It has been a regular storm.[14] My dear, it is in such times as you are now having that the voice of Jesus Christ can be best heard, 'Come into a desert place awhile.' Know you surely that it is God's visitation. Take home that thought, realise it:—God visiting you. Elizabeth was astonished that the Mother of her Lord should visit her. We can have our Emmanuel. I can look back on my sicknesses as the best times of my life. Don't fret about the future. He carrieth our sicknesses and healeth our infirmities. You know infirmity means weakness after sickness. Think of the cheering lines of our hymn: 'His touch has still its ancient power.' When I arose up from my sick-bed they told me I should never be able to enter a hospital or do work again. I was fretting over this when a good friend came to me, and told me only to take a day's burden and not look forward, and it was such a help. I got up every day feeling sure I should have strength and grace for the day's trial. May it be said of you, dear, 'They took knowledge of her that she had been with Jesus.' May He reveal Himself in all His beauty is the prayer of

"Your sincere friend,
"Sister Dora."

It does not truly represent Sister Dora to dwell on her outer life, and not look as well into that which is within, as it was the very mainspring of all her actions, as it, in fact, made her what she was.

The same writer to the Guardian gives some sentences from other letters:—

---

[13] H. M. J., in a letter to the Guardian, May 12th, 1880.
[14] A Yorkshire expression for heavy work.

144

"Take your cross day by day, dearie, and with Jesus Christ bearing the other end it will not be too heavy." "If we would find Jesus, it must be on the mountain, not in the plains or smooth places. 'He went up into a mountain and taught them, saying,' etc. It is only on a mountain-side that we shall see the Cross. It was only after Zacchæus had climbed the tree he could see Jesus. I have been thinking much of this lately. It is not in the smooth places we shall see Jesus, it is in the rough, in the storm, or by the sick-couch." "A Christian is one whose object is Christ." "I am rejoiced that you are enjoying Faber's hymns; they always warm me up. Oh! my dear, is it not sad that we prefer to live in the shade when we might have the glorious sunshine?"

It was during the winter of 1876-7 that Sister Dora felt the first approach of the terrible disease that was to cause her death, and then it was rather by diminution of strength than by actual pain. She consulted a doctor in Birmingham, in whom she placed confidence, and he told her the plain truth, that her days in this world were numbered. She exacted from him a pledge of secrecy, and then went on with her work as hitherto.

"She was suddenly brought," says Miss Lonsdale, "as it were, face to face with death—distant, perhaps, but inevitable: she, who was full of such exuberant life and spirits, that the very word 'death' seemed a contradiction when applied to her. Even her doctor, as he looked at her blooming appearance, and measured with his eye her finely made form, was almost inclined to believe the evidence of his outward senses against his sober judgment.... She could not endure pity. She, to whom everybody had learnt instinctively to turn for help and consolation, on whom others leant for support, must she now come down to ask of them sympathy and comfort? The pride of life was still surging up in her, that pride which had made her glory in her physical strength for its own sake, as well as for its manifold uses in the service of her Master. True, she had been long living two lives inseparably blended: the outward life, one of hard, unceasing toil; the inner, a constant communion with the unseen world, the existence of which she realised to an extent which not even those who saw the most of her could appreciate. To all the poor ignorant beings whose souls she tried to reach by means of their maimed bodies, she was, indeed, the personification of all that they could conceive as lovable, holy and merciful in the Saviour. At the same time she judged her own self with strict impartiality. She knew her own faults, her unbending will—her pride and glory in her work seemed to her even a fault; and, in place of looking on herself as perfect, she was bowed down with a sense of her own shortcomings. At the same time—with death before her, she hungered for more

145

work for her Master. His words were continually on her lips: 'I must work the works of Him that sent Me while it is day; the night cometh when no man can work.'"

At last, in the month of August, 1878, typhoid fever having broken out in the temporary hospital, it was found necessary to close it, and hasten on the work of the construction of another. This gave her an opportunity for a holiday and a complete change. She went to the Isle of Man, to London, and to Paris.

But the disorder was making rapid strides, and was causing her intense suffering, and she craved to be back at Walsall. She got as far as Birmingham, and was then in such a critical state, that it was feared she would die. But her earnest entreaty was to be taken to Walsall: "Let me die," she pleaded, "among my own people."

Mr. Welsh says:—"On calling at the Queen's Hotel, Birmingham [where she was lying ill], I was told the doctor of the hospital (Dr. Maclachlan) was with her, and thinking they were probably arranging matters connected with the hospital, I did not go to her room, but proceeded to the train. I had scarcely got seated when the doctor called me out, and we entered a compartment where we were alone. He asked me when it was intended to open the hospital. I replied, 'On the 4th November.' 'Then,' he said, 'that will just be about the time Sister Dora will die.'

"The announcement was to me a shock of no ordinary kind, for I had not heard of her being ill, and no one could have imagined, from the cheerful tone of a letter I had received from her a week or so before, that there was anything the matter with her. Not being able to fully realise the true state of affairs, I asked him if he were jesting. He replied he was not, and that he thought it best to let me know at once, so that arrangements might be made for getting some one to take her place when the hospital was opened. I said, 'I suppose she is going to Yorkshire?' 'No,' he replied, 'and that is another thing I wish to speak to you about. She wishes to die in Walsall, and she must be removed immediately.'

"On Sunday [the day following] I saw the chairman and vice-chairman of the hospital. On Sunday evening I returned with Dr. Maclachlan to the Queen's Hotel, where he found his patient very weak. On Monday morning, a house was taken, and the furniture she had in her rooms at the hospital removed to it. Her old servant, who had gone to The Potteries, was telegraphed for, and arrived in a few hours, and by midday the house was ready for her reception. My daughter, knowing Sister Dora's fondness for flowers, had procured and placed on the table in the parlour a very choice bouquet; and when all was ready, Dr. Maclachlan drove over to Birmingham, and brought her to Walsall in his private carriage.

146

"The disease was now making steady progress, and it was evident that every day she was becoming weaker; but she never lost her cheerfulness, and any one to have seen her might have thought she was only suffering from some slight ailment, instead of an incurable and painful disease."

"A few hours before her death," writes Mr. S. Welsh, "she called me to her bedside and said, 'I want you to promise that you will not, when I am gone, write anything about me; quietly I came among you, and quietly I wish to go away.'" And this desire of hers would have been faithfully complied with had not misrepresentations fired the gentleman to whom the request was made to take up his pen, not in defence of her, but in the correction of statements that affected certain persons who were alive. I must refer the reader for the detailed account of her last hours to Miss Lonsdale's book. One remarkable fact must not be omitted.

Among the members of the Basilian Order in the Eastern Church, it is the rule, as soon as one of the brothers or sisters is dying, that all should leave the room. The last office performed is to screw an ikon or representation of the Saviour to the foot of the bed, that the dying may in the supreme moment not think of any earthly tie, any earthly comfort, but look only to the Rock of his Salvation. Of this, Sister Dora knew nothing. In her last sickness she had a large crucifix hung where she could constantly gaze at it, and when she found her end approaching, she insisted on every one leaving the room,—it was her wish to die alone. And as she persisted, so was it, only one nurse standing by the door held ajar, and watching till she knew by the change of attitude, and a certain fixed look in the countenance, that Sister Dora had entered into her rest.[15]

Mr. Welsh says: "It was Christmas Eve when she passed away, and a dense fog, like a funeral pall, hung over the town and obscured every object a few feet from the ground. Under this strange canopy the market was being held, and people were busy buying and selling, and making preparations for the great Christmas Festival on the following day; but when the deep boom of the passing bell announced the melancholy intelligence that Sister Dora had entered into her rest, a thrill of horror ran through the people, who, with blanched cheeks and bated breath, whispered, 'Can it be true?' Although for eleven weeks the process of dissolution had been

---

[15] This has been denied. Her old and devoted servant said: "Do you think I would let my darling die alone?" But it appears to me that Sister Dora's desire was one to be expected in such a spiritual nature; and in the statement above given it is not said that she was actually left in solitude.

going on before their eyes, they could not realise the fact that she whom they loved and revered was no more."

The funeral took place on Saturday, the 28th of December. "The day was dark and dismal, the streets, covered with slush and sludge caused by the melted snow, were thronged with spectators.... There was general mourning in the town; and although it was market day nearly every shop was closed during the time of the funeral, and all the blinds along the route of the procession were drawn.... On reaching the cemetery it was found that four other funerals had arrived from the workhouse; and as these coffins had been taken into the chapel there was no room for Sister Dora's, which had consequently to be placed in the porch. This was as Sister Dora would have wished had she had the ordering of the arrangements; for she always gave preference to the poor, to whom she was attached in life, and from whom she would not have desired to be separated in death."

True to her thought of others, in the midst of her last sufferings she had made arrangements for a Christmas dinner to be given to a number of her old patients, in accordance with a custom of hers in previous years; but on this occasion the festive proceedings were shorn of their gladness. All thought of her who in her pain and on her deathbed had thought of them. Every one tried, but ineffectually, to cheer and comfort the other, but the task was hopeless. One young lady, after the meal, and while the Christmas tree was being lighted, commenced singing that pretty little piece, "Far Away,"—but when she came to the words,

"Some are gone from us for ever,
Longer here they could not stay,"

she burst into tears; and the women present sobbed, and tears were seen stealing down the cheeks of bearded men.

The Walsall writer of A Review concludes his paper thus:—

"She is no idol to us, but we worship her memory as the most saintly thing that was ever given to us. Her name is immortalized, both by her own surpassing goodness, and by the love of a whole people for her—a love that will survive through generations, and give a magic and a music to those simple words, 'Sister Dora,' long after we shall have passed away. There was little we could ever do— there was nothing she would let us do—to relieve the self-imposed rigours of her life; but we love her in all sincerity, and now in our helplessness we find a serene joy in the knowledge that to her, as surely as to any human soul, will be spoken the Divine words:

148

'Inasmuch as ye have done it unto the least of these My brethren, ye have done it unto Me.'"

In Sister Dora, surely we have the highest type of the Christian life, the inner and hidden life of the soul, the life that is hid with Christ in God, combined with that outer life devoted to the doing of good to suffering and needy humanity. In the cloistered nun we see only the first, and that tends to become self-centred and morbid; it is redeemed from this vice by an active life of self-sacrifice.

I cannot do better than, in conclusion, quote from the last letter ever penned by Sister Dora:—

"It is 2.30 a.m., and I cannot sleep, so I am going to write to you. I was anything but 'forbearing,' dear; I was overbearing, and I am truly sorry for it now. I look back on my life, and see 'nothing but leaves.' Oh, my darling, let me speak to you from my deathbed, and say, Watch in all you do that you have a single aim—God's honour and glory. 'I came not to work My own work, but the works of Him that sent Me.' Look upon working as a privilege. Do not look upon nursing in the way they do so much now-a-days, as an art or science, but as work done for Christ. As you touch each patient, think it is Christ Himself, and then virtue will come out of the touch to yourself. I have felt that myself, when I have had a particularly loathsome patient. Be full of the Glad Tidings, and you will tell others. You cannot give what you have not got."

9781647996109